Ancient China Trivia

Embark on a Captivating Journey Through Chinese History and Culture with 500 Intriguing Questions and Answers

Welcome Aboard, Check Out This Limited-Time Free Bonus!

Ahoy, reader! Welcome to the Ahoy Publications family, and thanks for snagging a copy of this book! Since you've chosen to join us on this journey, we'd like to offer you something special.

Check out the link below for a FREE e-book filled with delightful facts about American History.

But that's not all - you'll also have access to our exclusive email list with even more free e-books and insider knowledge. Well, what are ye waiting for? Click the link below to join and set sail toward exciting adventures in American History.

Access your bonus here

https://ahoypublications.com/

Or, Scan the QR code!

Table of Contents

Introduction

Ancient Chinese culture is one of the oldest and most intriguing cultures in the world. It was ahead of its time with its advanced inventions and inspiring philosophical views.

China became famous for its silk production. The Greeks and Romans called it "Seres" meaning "the land where silk comes from." Marco Polo referred to it as "Cat hay," and was the first person to introduce China to Europe.

This ancient culture is characterized by many dynasties that were born from farming communities and small villages. The trivia questions in this book take you on a journey through history, starting with Xia, the first dynasty. You will discover their myths and legends with some historical facts. The question will uncover Xia's mysteries.

You will learn about other dynasties such as the Zhou, Qin, Han, Tang, Song, and Ming, and their advancement in philosophy, poetry, and architecture. You will walk in the footsteps of ancient Chinese people with questions that challenge your imagination.

Ancient China was one of the most inventive civilizations worldwide. Their inventions and discoveries impacted Europe and the world. The trivia questions will open your horizons and help you apply creative thinking to understand the culture and its history.

The book then takes you on a spiritual journey with questions that encourage personal reflection and philosophical exploration.

One can't talk about ancient China without mentioning the Silk Road, Asia's most famous trading route. You will find questions that put you in the merchant's shoes to understand the challenges and decisions they face daily.

The trivia questions are fun, interactive, and fascinating. You won't only find True or False and multiple-choice questions but also role-play scenarios, decision-making scenarios, picture-based queries, and more. You'll find the answers in the Answer Key at the back of this book.

Are you ready to have fun, challenge yourself, and learn about ancient China?

Chapter 1: Dynastic Beginnings: Unveiling the Mysteries of Xia and Shang

Xia was ancient China's first and oldest dynasty and government and the first to start dynasty succession. For centuries, historians believed that it was a myth and didn't exist. However, in the 1960s and 1970s, archeologists discovered tombs, bronze works, and sites that could belong to the Xia Dynasty. Some scholars still think that the Xia Dynasty never existed, adding to its allure and linking it to legends and mythology.

The Shang Dynasty came next after overthrowing the Xia Dynasty. Historians who don't believe that the Xia dynasty existed agree that the Shang dynasty is the origin of Chinese culture. Ancient China thrived and developed during this time.

Historians question the existence of the Xia dynasty because they can't confirm whether the cities, they discovered belonged to them or the Shang dynasty since their architecture was similar.

Now that you have familiarized yourself with the Xia and Shang dynasties, test your knowledge with fun trivia questions.

True or False

1. The Shang Dynasty was known for its advanced use of bronze.
   - True
   - False

2. According to Chinese mythology, ancient China's first rulers resembled gods and had superpowers.
   - True
   - False

3. The Shang Dynasty didn't know how to use a calendar.
   - True
   - False

4. The Yellow River often flooded during the Xia Dynasty.
   - True
   - False

5. Chinese characters first appeared during the Xia Dynasty.
   - True
   - False

6. During the Xia Dynasty, the majority of ancient Chinese worked as farmers.
   - True
   - False

7. The Shang Dynasty invented musical instruments.
   - True
   - False

8. Yu the Great was a tyrant.
   - True
   - False

9. The Ming Dynasty replaced the Shang Dynasty.
   - True
   - False

10. People were only interested in agriculture during the Xia Dynasty.

- True
- False

Multiple Choice

How about making these multiple-choice questions more fun? Imagine you are a time traveler who has just landed in ancient China. You can travel through different timelines, which allows you to explore both the Xia Dynasty and the Shang Dynasty. You have a diary to write your thoughts and observations.

1. Diary entry: I wonder who was the Xia Dynasty's last ruler.

A. Qin

B. Ming

C. Jie

D. Zhou

2. Diary entry: I wonder how long the Shang Dynasty ruled China.

A. 50 years

B. 100 years

C. 550 years

D. 650 years

3. Diary entry: I wonder what happened to Gun after he failed to stop the flood.

A. He was awarded for his efforts

B. Yu Shun put him in prison

C. He retreated from public life and spent his days with his family

D. He disappeared, and no one knew what happened to him

4. Diary entry: I wonder which animals the Shang people used for oracle bones.

A. Whales and Leopards

B. Bears and otters

C. Wolves and monkeys

D. Oxen and turtles

5. Diary entry: I wonder who was Xia's longest ruler.

    A. Bu Jiang

    B. Emperor Qi

    C. Shao Kang

    D. Tai Kang

6. Diary entry: I wonder what the Shang people wrote on oracle bones.

    A. Ancient China's laws

    B. Questions

    C. People's names

    D. Magic spells

7. Diary entry: I wonder how many social classes were in ancient China during the Xia Dynasty.

    A. Three

    B. Four

    C. Five

    D. Six

8. Diary entry: I wonder what made archaeologists think that the Shang people believed in life after death.

    A. From the way the bodies were buried

    B. There were writings on the bones

    C. Studying pictures on tomb walls

    D. Finding weapons and food buried with kings

9. Diary entry: I wonder when the Xia Dynasty ended.

    A. 1600 B.C.

    B. 1500 B.C.

    C. 1400 B.C.

    D. 1200 B.C.

10. Diary entry: I wonder what Anyang was in the Shang Dynasty.

    A. Its longest ruler

    B. The capital city

    C. A religion

    D. Cheng Tang's wife

Fill in the Blanks

1. The legendary founder of the Xia dynasty was _____.
2. The Shang Dynasty was powerful because they had a strong _____.
3. The Xia Dynasty used agricultural tools made of _____ and _____.
4. The people the Shang armies captured during wars worked as _____.
5. The Xia king who introduced ancestor worship was _____.
6. The Shang supreme god was called _____.
7. Yu the Great divided China into _____ provinces.
8. The Xia Dynasty had _____ rulers.
9. The Xia ruler _____ introduced familial succession.
10. The _____ gave the Shang soldiers an advantage in battle.

Short Answers

1. Name one major archaeological site associated with the Shang Dynasty.

_____

_____

_____

2. What was Yu the Great famous for?

_____

_____

_____

3. If Xia didn't exist, who did historians believe invented it?

_____

_____

_____

4. Is the Shang Dynasty real or myth?

_____

_____

_____

5. Myth Vs. Fact: The Shang Kings were gods.

_____

_____

_____

6. Mention one question the Shang people wrote on oracle bones.

_____

_____

_____

7. Myth vs. Fact: No archeological sites prove the existence of the Xia Dynasty.

_____

_____

_____

8. What is the Yellow River called?

_____

_____

_____

9. What was the Shang economy built on?

_____

_____

_____

10. Myth Vs. Fact: Historians didn't hear of the Xia Dynasty until they discovered the Shang Dynasty.

_____

_____

_____

Picture-Based Query

1. Identify which dynasty this artifact belongs to and name one characteristic feature of its design.

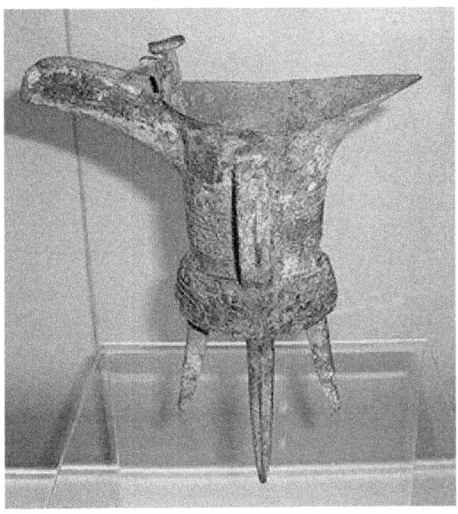

Illustration 1

Response: _____

2. Identify this image and which dynasty it belonged to.

Illustration 2

Response: _____

3. Name this ruler and identify which dynasty he belonged to.

人紀肇修　垂千萬垂
盤銘一德　永祚六事
以質繼忠　匪曰求異
順天應人　本乎仁義

湯

Illustration 3

Response: _____

4. Identify this picture and which dynasty it came from.

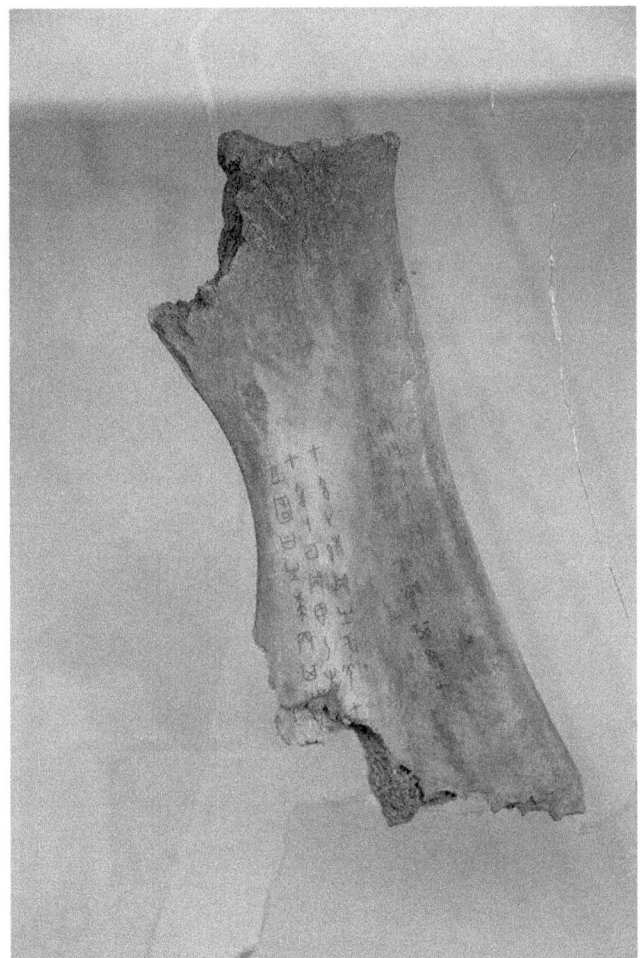

Illustration 4

Response: _____

5. Identify this image and the dynasty it came from.

Illustration 5

Response: _____

6. Identify this image and the dynasty it came from.

Illustration 6

Response: _____

7. Identify this image and the dynasty it came from.

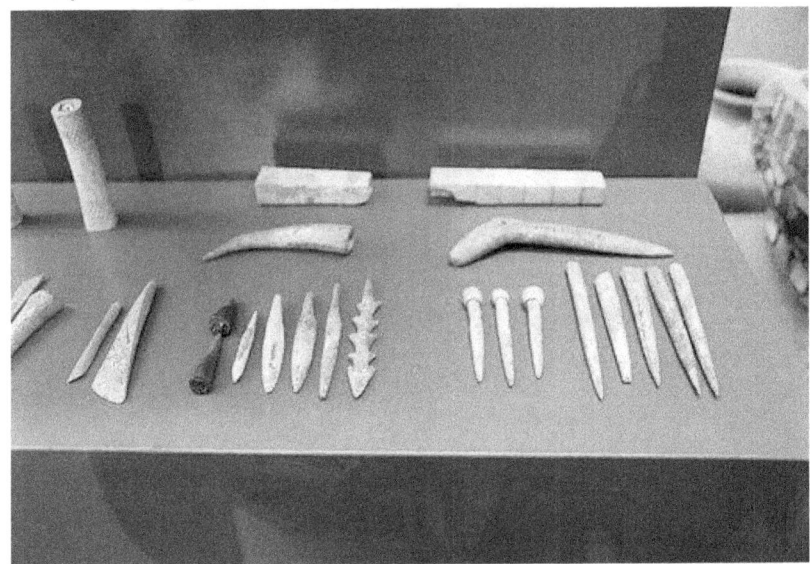

Illustration 7

Response: _____

8. Identify this image and the dynasty it came from.

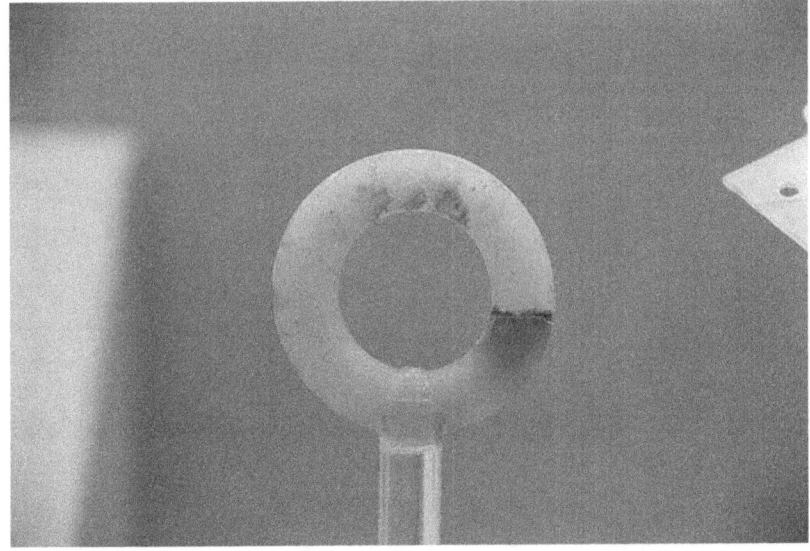

Illustration 8

Response: _____

9. Identify this image and the dynasty it came from.

Illustration 9

Response: _____

10. Identify this image.

Illustration 10

Response: _____

Answer Key

True or False Answers

1. **True** *(The Shang era is often called The Bronze Age of China because they used bronze to make ritual vessels, chariot parts, and weapons.)*

2. **True** *(According to a Chinese legend, ancient China's first rulers had god-like powers and helped create humans. It is believed that they invented farming, medicine, hunting, fishing, and writing. They ruled until the rise of the Xia Dynasty.)*

3. **False** *(During the Shang Dynasty, people had great knowledge of math and astronomy and even learned to use a calendar. A man named Wan-Nien developed a solar-based calendar with 365 days a year.)*

4. **True** *(The Yellow River flooded and disrupted agriculture. A man called Gun was described in many legends as a demi-god succeeded in controlling the flood. However, it was temporary. His son, Yu the Great, discovered a permanent solution. He built canals to direct the water to the sea to protect the people from the flood.)*

5. **False** *(Chinese characters first appeared during the Shang Dynasty. People often wrote on tortoise shells and cattle bones. They also had two numerological systems: 1-12 and 1-10.)*

6. **True** *(During the Xia Dynasty, people worked as farmers. They also invented irrigation, meaning watering the land with artificial methods.)*

7. **True** *(Musical instruments such as drums, bone flutes, chimes, and bells were invented during the Shang dynasty.)*

8. **False** *(Yu the Great protected people from the flood, which saved many from drowning and displacement. Many considered him a hero, yet he remained humble.)*

9. **False** *(The Zhou Dynasty brought the Shang Dynasty's downfall. Shang's last ruler, Di Xin, neglected his people and only focused on himself and his desires, which led to the Empire's falling apart.)*

10. **False** *(The Xia people created a variety of metalwork, and they used bronze to make weapons and art.)*

Multiple Choice Answers

1. **C. Jie** *(Jie was a cruel and tyrant ruler whose drinking, ill-advised decisions, and bad behavior led to the fall of the Xia Dynasty.)*

2. **C. 550 years** *(The Shang Dynasty stayed in power for 500-550 years. During which they invented writing, advanced in Bronze technology, and formed a government.)*

3. **B. Yu Shun put him in prison** *(It is believed that either Yu Shun put him in prison or he exiled himself in the mountains.)*

4. **D. Oxen and turtles** *(The Shang people used oxen bones and turtle shells to practice divination, which helped them see the future and gain knowledge)*

5. **A. Bu Jiang** *(Bu Jiang ruled the Xia Dynasty for 59 years, and he was known for his wisdom. He passed the throne to his younger brother Jiong in his 59th year and died ten years later.)*

6. **B. Questions** *(Sang diviners or priests would send questions to the gods, asking them about the weather, plants, or the future. The oracle bones archeologists found are about 3500 years old.)*

7. **B. Four** *(There are four social classes in the Xia Dynasty: Slaves, farmers, craftsmen, and aristocracy.)*

8. **D. Finding weapons and food buried with kings** *(Ancient cultures that believed in the afterlife buried their royals and other important figures with objects they believed they might need in the other world, such as weapons, food, and bronze.)*

9. **A. 1600 B.C.** *(Xia's last ruler, Jie, was a tyrant who caused the dynasty's downfall. Cheng Tang overthrew him and started the Shang Dynasty.)*

10. **B. The capital city** *(Yin Xu was the Shang Dynasty's capital, and it was near Anyang, the first stable Chinese city. However, some people refer to Anyang as Shang Dynasty's capital.)*

Fill in the Blanks Answers

1. **Yu the Great** *(He was one of the descendants of the Yellow Emperor who created Chinese culture. Many still believe that Yu was a mythical figure, but some historical findings indicate that he might have existed and was able to stop the flood.)*

2. **Army** *(The Shang Dynasty had a powerful and organized army. They were also equipped with highly sophisticated weapons such*

as bronze spearheads and swords, which were stronger than the weapons their opponents used. This gave them the edge in battle.)

3. **Stone and bones** (*Although bronze was commonly used during the Xia Dynasty, farmers' daily tools were made of bone and stone.*)

4. **Slaves** (*Prisoners of war were either killed or enslaved in the Shang Dynasty.*)

5. **Shao Kang** (*Shao Kang was the Xia Dynasty's sixth king and one of its greatest rulers. Ancestor worship is an ancient religious belief that is based on respecting the dead. It is believed that when a family member dies, they become close to the gods and can harm or help the living.*)

6. **Shangdi** (*Shangdi was the most important ancient Chinese deity. He was responsible for floods, harvest, and victory in battle. Only kings could communicate with him through the spirits of their ancestors.*)

7. **Nine** (*The nine provinces were Ji, Yan, Qing, Xu, Yang, Jing, Yu, Yong, and Liang.*)

8. **Seventeen** (*Xia Dynasty had 17 kings. However, many of them were oppressive, cruel, and tyrants, such as Jie, and some were brave and just, such as Yu the Great*).

9. **Yu the Great** (*Yu the Great named his son Qi to be his successor on his deathbed. Before, Chinese emperors were chosen based on their skills and abilities. By choosing his son, Yu started the Xia Dynasty. Future rulers followed his lead and chose one of their sons or a family member to be their successor before their death.*)

10. **Chariot** (*The Shang army had many advanced weapons, but the chariot was their most powerful war invention. They domesticated horses, but they were too small to ride, so they used the chariot to harness the horses' strength. It allowed the soldiers to move and travel faster than their enemies.*)

Short Answers

1. **Yin Xu** (*Yin Xu is located in south Beijing and began ancient China's golden age, which witnessed advancement in sciences and crafts. It is home to ancient Chinese palaces, tombs, royal shrines, and more.*)

2. **Stopping the flood** (*Stopping the flood was Yu's greatest accomplishment. It is said that he refused to return home until he*

finished the project, which lasted for 13 years. He even passed by his house three times, and his wife and child would call out to him, but he didn't answer them. His colleagues pleaded with him to go home and rest, but he refused. He said that the flood killed many people and made many families homeless, so he wasn't going to rest until everyone was safe.)

3. **The Zhou Dynasty** (Some scholars think that Xia wasn't a real dynasty. The Zhou Dynasty's rulers wanted to convince the people that previous dynasties had fallen because their kings were immoral. They used the Xia Dynasty as an example of kingdoms that declined because their rulers didn't follow heaven's rules.)

4. **Real** (For centuries, scholars couldn't prove that the Shang Dynasty existed. However, they discovered inscriptions on oracle bones that match texts that were written centuries later, proving that the Shang Dynasty was real.)

5. **Myth** (The Shang wasn't a mythical city, and its kings were normal human beings, but they believed they were divine rulers who could connect to their ancestors)

6. **"Will we win the war?"** (The Shang people asked the gods different questions, such as whether a disease would be cured, whether a farming season would be successful, or military-related questions. They also asked personal questions such as if they would have a son, whether they should go on a hunting trip or not, or if their loved one would accept their marriage proposal.)

7. **Myth** (Archaeologists found remains of barns and a palace in Henan in Central China from 4000 years ago. They believe that the Xinmi ancient city site and the Zhuqiu Temple belonged to the Xia Dynasty.)

8. **Cradle of Civilization** (The Yellow River was given that name because China's oldest dynasties were built around it. It also goes by other names such as Mother River, the Huang He River, and China's Pride and China's Sorrow because, during floods, it killed many people.)

9. **Agriculture** (The Shang Dynasty's economy was built on artisanship, agriculture, and trade, but agriculture was the dynasty's economic backbone.)

10. **Myth** (Historians discovered the Xia Dynasty from ancient Chinese writings such as the Records of the Grand Historian and

the Classic of History.)

Picture-Based Query Answers

1. **Shang/made of bronze** *(Many bronze vessels represent respect and power in the Shang Dynasty. Each piece has unique characteristics, which make them more fascinating. Royals used these vessels in various rituals.)*

2. **Chariot/Shang Dynasty** *(Ancient Chinese chariots only had two wheels and were drawn by two horses. They were made of bronze, cane, rattan, bamboo, and wood. Chariots are often present in many burial sites. They were used more for hunting, ceremonies, and to give emperors prestige.)*

3. **King Tang of Shang** *(King Tang established the Shang Dynasty by leading a revolution against Xia's tyrant King Jie. He was brave enough to stand up and protest his ill-treatment of the Chinese people. His last battle against the Xia ruler was called the "Battle of Mingtiao," which resulted in Jie's defeat.)*

4. **Oracle bones from the Shang Dynasty** *(They are also called dragon bones. The carved symbols became recognizable Chinese characters. Fortune tellers would write or paint words on a turtle shell or an animal bone and heat it until it cracked. They used the crack's direction to tell the future. Although other dynasties used oracle bones to predict the future, the practice was more common during the Shang Dynasty.)*

5. **Pottery from the Xia Dynasty** *(Xia pottery is characterized by being practical and simple. It was made of brown or gray clay. Many were decorated with geometric patterns. They used pottery to make dishes, bowls, jars, and other daily items.)*

6. **Helmets from the Shang Dynasty** *(The Shang were known for having a powerful military and advanced weapons. The helmets were high-quality and made of bronze to protect the dynasty's warriors.)*

7. **Bone artifacts from the Shang Dynasty** *(The Shang people used bones to make various artifacts that they could use daily for cooking, fishing, or hunting, such as harpoons and spearheads. They also used them to make hairpins that women used every day.)*

8. **Jade ring from the Shang Dynasty** *(Jade is a type of stone that was popular among Shang nobles and kings. They put jade rings with the dead in their tombs to protect the body from decay. The stone was associated with the rich.)*

9. **Stone cowries from the Shang Dynasty** *(The stone cowries were considered valuable objects and a sign of wealth.)*

10. **The Yellow River** *(It is the birthplace of ancient Chinese civilization, which is why it is called the "Mother River.")*

Chapter 2: Philosophies, Feudalism, and the Warring States

The Zhou Dynasty was one of the most important dynasties in ancient China. It came after the decline of the Shang Dynasty and was followed by the Qin Dynasty. The Shang and the Zhou Dynasties share many similarities. They also introduced different philosophies and concepts to set themselves apart from other dynasties.

This chapter covers fun and intriguing trivia about the Zhou Dynasty.

True or False

1. **The Zhou Dynasty was divided into two periods.**

   - True
   - False

2. **The Zhou Dynasty was the longest-lasting dynasty in Chinese history.**

   - True
   - False

3. **The Mandate of Heaven was introduced before the Zhou Dynasty.**

   - True
   - False

4. The Zhou Dynasty fell because its last ruler was a drunk and a tyrant.

- True
- False

5. The Zhou Dynasty ruled China using the feudal system.

- True
- False

6. The Zhou Dynasty only used bronze to make their weapons.

- True
- False

7. Eastern Zhou came before Western Zhou.

- True
- False

8. Ceramic artifacts were popular during the Zhou Dynasty.

- True
- False

9. Buddhist philosophy began during the Zhou Dynasty.

- True
- False

10. Ancient Chinese people continued worshiping Shangdi throughout the Zhou Dynasty.

- True
- False

Multiple Choice

1. What are the similarities between the Shang Dynasty and the Zhou Dynasty?

A. The practice of divination

B. The use of bronze ritual vessels

C. Religious rituals

D. All of the above

2. What metal was introduced during the Zhou Dynasty?

   A. Silver

   B. Iron

   C. Gold

   D. Bronze

3. Which describes a period when multiple Chinese states battled against each other for territorial gain?

   A. Golden Age of China

   B. Xia Dynasty

   C. Warring States Period

   D. Shang Dynasty

4. What is the name of the battle where the Zhou's army defeated the Shang's army?

   A. The Battle of Zhou

   B. The Battle of Yang

   C. The Yellow River Battle

   D. The Battle of Muye

5. What did famine and natural disasters mean according to the Mandate of Heaven?

   A. The end of the world

   B. There won't be any harvest this year

   C. The emperor failed and should be replaced

   D. No children will be born this year

6. Who was called "The Son of Heaven"?

   A. A famous poet

   B. A mythical hero

   C. A brave warrior

   D. Zhou's rulers

7. How many classes was the Zhou Dynasty divided into?

   A. Three

   B. Four

   C. Five

   D. Six

8. According to the "Mandate of Heaven," when could the people overthrow their ruler?

    A. When he couldn't have children

    B. When he ruled unfairly

    C. When he started to lose his memory

    D. When the people found a better ruler

9. What did the Zhou call heaven?

    A. Tian

    B. Yang

    C. Wu

    D. Zeus

10. What was the Eastern Zhou period called?

    A. Summer and winter

    B. Spring and Autumn

    C. Yin and Yang

    D. Black and white

Fill in the Blanks

1. The philosophy that there should only be one ruler chosen by the gods is called _____.

2. The majority of the people from the Zhou Dynasty were _____.

3. The Zhou Dynasty believed that the _____ had lost the Mandate of Heaven.

4. The farmlands belonged to the _____.

5. The Zhou Dynasty's biggest achievement was _____.

6. The most famous Daoist teacher was _____.

7. The philosophy that encourages living in harmony with nature is called _____.

8. The Zhou Dynasty improved trade by using _____ and _____.

9. Ancient China entered the _____ during the Zhou Dynasty.

10. The famous book _____ by Sun Tzu was written during the Zhou Dynasty.

Short Answers

1. Name one major contribution of Confucianism to Chinese society.

_____

_____

_____

2. What are Confucius's five virtues?

_____

_____

_____

3. Which philosophies were created during the Zhou Dynasty?

_____

_____

_____

4. Why did Confucius think China should return to ethics?

_____

_____

_____

5. Name an important weapon the Zhou people invented during the Warring States period.

_____

_____

_____

Philosopher's Corner

1. Do you believe people are born evil and selfish and should be controlled with strict laws?

_____

_____

_____

2. Do you think that the feudal system is a fair ruling system?

_____

_____

_____

3. Do you agree with Confucius that you should love everyone?

_____

_____

_____

4. Do you believe that all people can be good?

_____

_____

_____

5. Do you believe that everything in the universe is connected, even good and bad?

_____

_____

_____

Picture-Based Query

1. Name this important figure.

周武王 （？ 一前1042 ） 明人绘

Illustration 11

Response: _____.

2. Identify the dynasty these coins are from and discuss one key economic activity during that period.

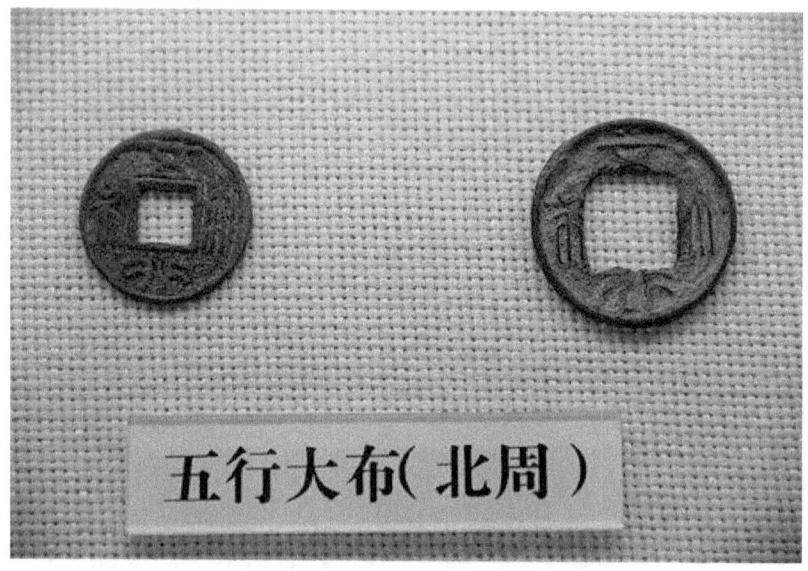

五行大布(北周)

Illustration 12

Response: _____

3. Identify this object and mention what it was used for.

Illustration 13

Response: _____

4. Name this famous philosopher and mention one of his famous quotes.

Illustration 14

Response: _____

5. Identify the period this ceramic stoneware is from.

Illustration 15

Response: _____

6. Name this weapon, what it was made of, and which period it came from.

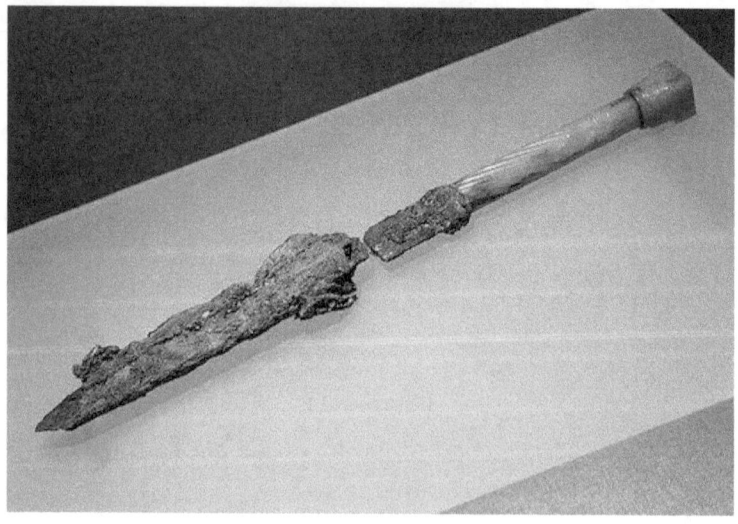

Illustration 16

Response: _____

7. Name this famous philosopher and mention one fact about him.

Illustration 17

Response: _____

8. Which dynasty does that artifact belong to? Mention the importance of these inscriptions.

Illustration 18

Response: _____

9. Identify this picture and mention what it was made of.

Illustration 19

Response: _____

10. Identify the dynasty this artifact came from and what it was made of.

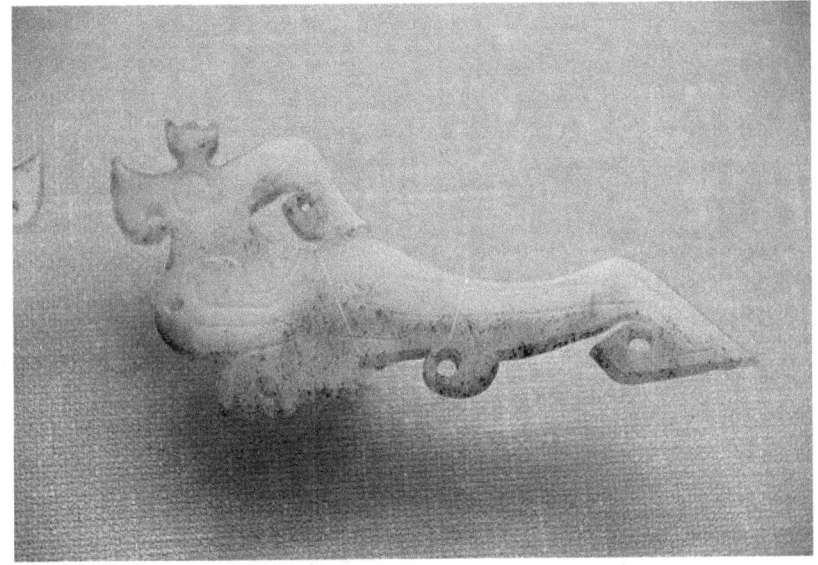

Illustration 20

Response: _____.

Answer Key

1. **True** *(The Zhou Dynasty is divided into the Western Zhou, which lasted from 1046 to 771 BCE, and Eastern Zhou from 771 to 256 BCE. The Western Zhou period witnessed the beginning of feudalism, which was common in many European countries. Feudalism is a system in which the nobles gave farmers and peasants lands and protection, and in return, they worked and fought for the upper class. The Eastern Zhou came after the Western period ended and followed its model. However, in time, there were several wars between the Chinese states, which resulted in the Warring States period.)*

2. **True** *(The Zhou Dynasty lasted for 789 years from 1046 to 256 B.C.E. Many reasons contributed to its longevity. Adopting the feudal system brought stability to the country. During this time, China underwent multiple changes and innovations. New advances in irrigation took place, enhancing farming and opening the door for more people to migrate to the country).*

3. **False** *(The Mandate of Heaven was created during the Zhou Dynasty. It was a divine source that gave Chinese kings the right to rule. The Zhou god Tian chose the right ruler, and only one legitimate king at a time should rule. The emperor should have honorable qualities and strong morals and ethics. The Zhou created the Mandate of Heaven to justify overthrowing the Shang Dynasty, whose last king was unjust and cruel and neglected his duties.)*

4. **False** *(The Zhou Dynasty fell apart gradually for various reasons. The feudal system played a big role in the dynasty's decline. The king gave lands to his family members or noblemen. This helped the king maintain control over China as people he trusted were governing different parts of the country. However, these lands turned into states and started gaining power, leading to the Warring States period, which lasted for centuries. The Qin Dynasty took advantage of China's division, conquered the country, and ended the Zhou Dynasty.)*

5. **True** *(The emperor gave lands to people he trusted, and they allowed peasants to work on them. However, feudalism didn't*

work in ancient China as it weakened the emperor's authority, leading to the end of the Zhou Dynasty.)

6. **False** *(The Zhou Dynasty used bronze and iron to make weapons. Although the Shang Dynasty also used iron, the Iron Age didn't start until the other half of the Zhou Dynasty).*

7. **False** *(Ancient Chinese lived in peace during the Western Zhou period. However, when the nobles became powerful and rebelled against the king, his son escaped to Luoyang, which became the Eastern Zhou capital.)*

8. **True** *(Ceramics played a big role in ancient Chinese culture, and artisans created many ceramic artifacts such as altar pots and burial urns)*

9. **False** *(Many philosophical schools emerged during the Zhou Dynasty. People started to think differently and changed the way they lived and saw the world. The Mandate of Heaven is the biggest example of how the ancient Chinese adopted new thoughts and beliefs. Confucius and Lao Tzu also introduced new philosophies that had a huge impact on the Zhou society. However, Buddhism didn't start in China until the Han Dynasty in the fifth century.)*

10. **False** *(Ancient Chinese worshiped Shangdi during the Western Zhou period. The Shang Dynasty influenced the Zhou's religious beliefs. However, over time, they moved away from the Shang beliefs and created their own by worshiping their god, Tian.)*

Multiple Choice Answers

1. **D. All of the above** *(The Shang and Zhou dynasties shared many similarities, especially during the Western Zhou period. Both practiced divination, used bronze ritual vessels and performed religious rituals. They were also farmers and worked on advancing irrigation).*

2. **B. Iron** *(After the Zhou Dynasty conquered the Shang Dynasty and took control of the country, they entered an era of innovation and advanced technology by using iron to create powerful weapons).*

3. **C. The Warring States Period** *(In the fifth century, the Eastern Zhou Dynasty was falling apart. It was getting weaker while the other states were growing stronger. The East couldn't depend on its army; it wasn't as powerful as it used to be, and it had to depend*

on other states for military support. These states took advantage of the situation to expand their territories. In the fourth century, 100 small states joined together and created seven major states: Zhao, Yan, Wei, Qin, Qi, Han, and Chu. They became so powerful, separated themselves from the Zhou Dynasty, and each had its own king. The seven states wanted to grow their power and expand their territories, so they attacked each other, leading to 358 wars, which gave the period its name.)

4. **D. The Battle of Muye** (*It was one of the biggest and most important battles in China's history, ending with Zhou's victory and the establishment of the Zhou Dynasty. It was a difficult war that lasted for years. King Wu of Zhou was outnumbered, but he was also a clever army general with effective tactics and strategies, which gave him an advantage.*)

5. **C. The king failed and should be replaced** (*The king should have many positive qualities to be a ruler in ancient China. However, if he became cruel and a tyrant, the gods would send famine and natural disasters as a sign that the king should be replaced.*)

6. **D. Zhou's ruler** (*According to the Mandate of Heaven, the Chinese king was called the "Son of Heaven" because the gods chose him.*)

7. **A. Three** (*Feudalism divided society into emperors, nobles, and peasants. Each class should serve the other. The emperor gave lands to the nobles, who, in return, provided him with military support. The peasants paid the nobles with services and goods to let them use the lands.*)

8. **B. When he ruled unfairly** (*The Mandate of Heaven is sacred, and its rules are clear. The king didn't have to be of noble birth; he should be moral, just, and good. If he became a tyrant, he would lose the Mandate of Heaven and should be overthrown*).

9. **A. Tian** (*Tian means heaven and god, and it is one of the oldest Chinese words. Ancient Chinese believed that Tian brought justice and peace to mankind through the ruler, and he was the only person who could communicate with god and heaven*).

10. **B. Spring and Autumn** (*The Spring and Autumn period was from 771 to 476 BCE, and it refers to a time before the Warring States when the king started to lose power and the feudal states grew stronger. This period was also called the "Hundred Schools of Thought" because many philosophers, such as Confucius,*

appeared during that time.

Fill in the Blanks Answer

1. **Mandate of Heaven** *(That ruler was the most powerful man on Earth and had many responsibilities toward his people.)*

2. **Peasants** *(The peasants had a hard life and were forced to serve in the army, but the nobles protected them from the dynasty's enemies.)*

3. **Shang Dynasty** *(The Zhou Dynasty believed that the Shang Dynasty had to be overthrown because their last king was cruel and a tyrant who tortured his people. He wasn't fit to rule because he wasn't just or worthy to be called "Son of Heaven.")*

4. **Loyal nobles** *(During the Zhou Dynasty, China expanded, and the king couldn't govern it alone, so he gave lands to nobles he trusted, and they swore loyalty to him.)*

5. **Cast iron** *(The invention of cast iron changed the Zhou Dynasty and ancient China. It helped them make durable and powerful tools and weapons that strengthened their army).*

6. **Lao Tzu** *(Lao Tzu was the father of Daoism or Taoism. He is one of the most famous philosophers in the world. He was called "Old Master" or "Old Man." Some historians believe that Tzu never existed and that the name Lao Tzu represented a blend of different philosophers. They agree that he was a mythical figure who symbolized the idea of a spiritual teacher. People who follow the Taoism religion consider him a god. However, according to Chinese tradition, he existed in the sixth century.)*

7. **Taoism** *(Taoism is an ancient Chinese philosophy that was influenced by Chinese folk religious beliefs. It became the country's official religion during the Tang Dynasty. It teaches people to go with the flow and do what feels natural to them.)*

8. **Roads and coins** *(The Zhou Dynasty used metal coins and created more roads to improve trade in China. The roads helped merchants distribute resources and goods among Chinese states. The success of trade made merchants wealthy, and they took advantage of peasants so they would work for them.)*

9. **Iron Age** *(The Iron Age began in ancient China during the period between the Spring and Autumn and the Warring States.)*

10. **The Art of War** *(The book was written in the fifth century during the Zhou Dynasty. Sun Tzu was a Chinese military general and strategist. Like Lao Tzu, historians debate his existence. What they know is that someone existed during this time and wrote The Art of War. It is one of the most influential books about war and contains information about finding the enemy's location, military tactics, and more.)*

Short Answers

1. **Ethics and morals** *(Confucius was one of China's most important philosophers and teachers. Many books were written about his thoughts on ethics, morals, and good behavior. Confucianism stresses the importance of being a good person and how it affects others and the world around them. For example, kings should be kind and have good morals if they want their rule to be peaceful. His thoughts are similar to the Mandate of Heaven. He even mentioned that natural disasters happen when rulers and people ignore the teachings of their ancestors. He said a good person should be humble, respectful, and selfless.)*

2. **Fidelity (loyalty), propriety (decency), wisdom, righteousness, and benevolence (kindness)** *(Confucius believed that each person should have these five virtues, whether a king or a peasant. People who followed these virtues in ancient China were admired and respected.)*

3. **Confucianism, Taoism, and Legalism** *(Legalism is an ancient Chinese philosophical belief. It explains that when people are given a choice between right and wrong, they will choose to do the wrong thing because they are selfish and need strict laws to control their behavior. Han Feizi, the creator of Legalism, thought differently than Confucius; he believed that people are good by nature. Han believed that humans were born evil and should be punished when they broke the law. Taoism is about humans and animals living in harmony or balance with the universe. Confucianism encourages education because it helps people grow and be better. Confucianism is both a philosophy and a religion. However, unlike Taoism, people don't consider Confucius a god but a spiritual guide. This is why some people argue that Confucianism isn't a religion.)*

4. To restore order *(Confucius believed that people should return to the five virtues by learning philosophy, literature, and history and use what they learned to become better people and rulers. When everyone had good ethics, order would be restored in the universe, and they would live in peace and harmony.)*

5. Crossbow *(The Zhou people invented the crossbow during the Warring States period. It was ancient China's most important weapon and played a big role in the Chinese states' victory against their enemies. The Eastern Zhou Dynasty was famous for having powerful soldiers who trained for years to use a crossbow. They could walk for a hundred miles without rest. It was believed that one good crossbowman was better than 100 soldiers.)*

Picture-Based Query Answers

1. King Wu of Zhou *(He was the Zhou Dynasty's founder and ruled China for about three years. Wu introduced feudalism to ancient Chinese by distributing lands among his 16 brothers and other family members.)*

2. Zhou Dynasty/trading *(Zhou used coins to make trading easier and fair.)*

3. Spearhead/used for battle *(The Western Zhou Dynasty was established during the Bronze Age, and they made many weapons from bronze, such as war chariots, shields, bows and arrows, spears, and swords).*

4. Confucius *"Do not do to others what you do not want them to do to you."*

5. Warring States Period *(Ancient Chinese used many ceramics to make stoneware vessels, unpainted earthenware, and more.)*

6. Iron sword from the Western Zhou Dynasty *(The Zhou Dynasty took advantage of the Iron Age by making many powerful and advanced weapons that increased their power.)*

7. Lao Tzu *(He had a son called Zong, who became a brave and powerful soldier and defeated many of his enemies.)*

8. Western Zhou Dynasty *(The inscriptions on the artifacts help historians learn about the Zhou Dynasty.)*

9. Bronze helmet *(This helmet was from the Warring States period, and it shows that the Zhou dynasty used both bronze and iron to make weapons.)*

10. Jade artifact from the Western Zhou Dynasty *(Jade was used during the Zhou Dynasty to make various ritualistic objects.)*

Chapter 3: Imperial Majesty: The Qin and Han Dynastic Achievements

Imperial China was a period that witnessed the rise and fall of many dynasties. It was a stable time in China's history. The Qin Dynasty was Imperial China's first dynasty. Its rulers learned so much from their predecessors and changed the country's political system to avoid the same pitfalls. However, they made terrible mistakes, which led to severe consequences.

The Han Dynasty was the second Imperial Chinese dynasty. Its founder worked hard to fix the Qin rulers' mistakes. It was famous for its many inventions, some of which changed the world.

Each dynasty is characterized by its own culture, religion, philosophy, beliefs, and history. Many foreign politics and cultures influenced these dynasties, and the country thrived during this time in art, literature, architecture, technology, and more.

Now, get ready to answer some fun trivia questions and learn more about the Qin and Han Dynasties.

True or False

1. The Qin Dynasty ended the feudal system by reducing the nobles' power.
   - True
   - False

2. The Qin Dynasty is the shortest ancient Chinese dynasty.
   - True
   - False

3. The founder of the Han Dynasty was an aristocrat.
   - True
   - False

4. The Han Dynasty was divided into two periods.
   - True
   - False

5. The Han Dynasty was known for the invention of paper.
   - True
   - False

6. The Qin Dynasty used Legalism.
   - True
   - False

7. The Qin Dynasty encouraged people to get an education.
   - True
   - False

8. The Qin Dynasty lost the Mandate of Heaven.
   - True
   - False

9. The Qin Dynasty unified China by enforcing the same religion.
   - True
   - False

10. The Han Dynasty is called the Golden Age.

- True
- False

Multiple Choice

1. What was the Qin Dynasty's biggest achievement?

A. Making advanced iron weapons

B. Unifying the separated states after the Warring States period

C. Making a new Mandate of Heaven

D. Stopping the Yellow River floods

2. Who was the founder of the Han Dynasty?

A. Liu Bang

B. Liu Han

C. Liu Qin

D. Wuwan of Han

3. The Han Dynasty restored the values of which Dynasty?

A. The Xia Dynasty

B. The Shang Dynasty

C. The Zhou Dynasty

D. The Qin Dynasty

4. What was the primary purpose of the Great Wall of China?

A. Royal decoration

B. Flood control

C. Defense against invasions

D. Religious ceremonies

5. What religion was introduced during the Han Dynasty?

A. Christianity

B. Taoism

C. Buddhism

D. All of the above

6. What religion did the Qin Dynasty believe in?

    A. Taoism

    B. Confucianism

    C. Christianity

    D. They didn't believe in any religion

7. How many classes were in the Han Dynasty?

    A. Three

    B. Four

    C. Five

    D. Six

8. Which dynasty interrupted the Han Dynasty?

    A. Qin Dynasty

    B. Xin Dynasty

    C. Tang Dynasty

    D. Sing Dynasty

9. How did Buddhism spread to China?

    A. It was passed from the Qin Dynasty to the Han Dynasty

    B. By Buddhist monks traveling from India

    C. By famous philosophers

    D. The Chinese read about it in books

10. How were people chosen for government work during the Han Dynasty?

    A. They had to have knowledge of Confucius's work

    B. They had to be nobles

    C. They had to be related to the king

    D. They had to be rich

Fill in the Blanks

1. The first emperor of the Qin Dynasty was _____.

2. _____ weren't respected during the Han Dynasty.

3. The organization that was founded during the Han Dynasty and lasted for 2000 years was called _____.

4. The Silk Road was invented during the _____.

5. After the Qin Dynasty emperor died and his son came to power, _____.

6. The Qin Dynasty had _____ government.

7. _____ was the main philosophy during the Han Dynasty.

8. Shi Huangdi means _____.

9. The Xin Dynasty emperor was called _____.

10. The Silk Road was from _____ to _____.

Short Answers

Make this more interesting by imagining Emperor Shi Huang is giving you these challenges. Answer fast because this man is a tyrant and doesn't have much patience!

1. I challenge you to mention the major achievements of the Han Dynasty in the field of science.

_____

_____

_____

2. I challenge you to tell me why the Chinese invented the seismograph.

_____

_____

_____

3. I challenge you to mention an interesting fact about me (Shi Huangdi.)

_____

_____

_____

4. I challenge you to tell me why the Qin Dynasty burned books.

_____

_____

_____

5. I challenge you to tell me why the Qin Dynasty didn't follow Confucianism.

_____

_____

_____

6. I challenge you to give me a reason for what made the Han Dynasty different from its predecessors.

_____

_____

_____

7. I challenge you to mention one benefit of the invention of paper.

_____

_____

_____

8. I challenge you to tell me who the longest-reigning Han emperor was.

_____

_____

_____

9. I challenge you to tell me what Buddha meant by this quote, "Peace comes from within. Do not seek it without."

_____

_____

_____

10. I challenge you to tell me what the biggest products were in the Han Dynasty.

_____

_____

_____

Picture-Based Query

1. Identify which dynasty these sculptures are associated with and what their significance is in Chinese history.

Illustration 21

Response: _____.

2. Identify this picture and mention which dynasty it is associated with.

Illustration 22

Response: _____.

3. Name this famous emperor and the Dynasty to which he belonged.

Illustration 23

Response: _____.

4. Identify this picture and the dynasty it's associated with.

Illustration 24

Response: _____.

5. Name this famous ruler and the dynasty to which he belonged.

Illustration 25

Response: _____.

6. Name this famous figure and mention one of his quotes.

Illustration 26

Response: _____.

7. Which dynasty is this painting from?

Illustration 27

Response: _____.

8. Which dynasty does the statue of Queen Mother of the West belong to?

Illustration 28

Response: _____.

9. Which dynasty does this watchtower belong to?

Illustration 29

Response: _____.

10. Which dynasty does this chariot ornament belong to?

Illustration 30

Response: _____.

Answer Key

1. **True** *(The Qin Dynasty conquered the separated Zhou states and rose to power. Qin's emperor learned from the mistakes of the previous dynasty and didn't give much power to the nobles or aristocrats. He got rid of the feudal system that caused the Warring States period and destroyed the Zhou Dynasty.)*

2. **True** *(The Qin Dynasty only lasted for 15 years because the first emperor was a tyrant. When he died, the people revolted against his son, and chaos spread across the country until the Han Dynasty rose to power.)*

3. **False** *(Liu Bang, the founder of the Han Dynasty, was a peasant and made history by becoming the first commoner to form a Chinese dynasty.)*

4. **True** *(The Han Dynasty was divided into Western Han from 202 BCE to 9 CE and Eastern Han from 25 to 220 CE. The Xin Dynasty caused this division when it rose to power for a short time.)*

5. **True** *(Cai Lun invented paper in 105 A.D. He was a Chinese man working at the king's court. He used different ingredients for his invention, such as mulberry tree bark, fishing nets, rags, hemp, and bamboo. He pounded them, mixed them with water, and spread them flat. Paper became very popular among the Chinese people.)*

6. **True** *(The Qin Dynasty applied the Legalism philosophy and reinforced harsh laws and living conditions. Legalism's main principles included a strong legal system, the belief that people are selfish by nature, and harsh punishments to force people to be loyal to the king).*

7. **False** *(The Qin emperor prevented people from getting an education to make it easier to control them).*

8. **True** *(The Qin's first emperor lost the Mandate of Heaven because he was a cruel tyrant who made the people's lives hard. The rich and poor struggled to live under his rule. He destroyed the nobles and took away their power, burned books which made scholars hate him, and forced the peasants to work without pay.)*

9. **False** *(The Qin Dynasty unified China by using the same written language, applying the same rules and punishments, and introducing a uniform copper coin across the country.)*

10. **True** *(The Han Dynasty was called the golden age because it was a peaceful time when the empire expanded, and Confucianism was developed.)*

Multiple Choice Answers

1. **B. Unifying the separated states after the Warring States period** *(The Qin Dynasty unified China for the first time in its history instead of spreading its lands and powers among multiple states.)*

2. **A. Liu Bang** *(Liu's parents were peasants, but after Qin's first emperor died, he joined the rebels against the Qin Dynasty. He fought hard against the tyrants until the Han Dynasty rose to power, and he became its emperor. According to ancient Chinese legend, Liu was born after his mother dreamt of a dragon. It is believed that he was a descendant of the mythical figure, the Yellow Emperor.)*

3. **C. The Zhou Dynasty** *(The Qin Dynasty tried to erase all the Zhou Dynasty's achievements from history. They also moved away from any of their political and philosophical beliefs, such as feudalism and Confucianism. When the Han Dynasty rose to power, they restored many of the Zhou Dynasty's cultural values and philosophical thinking. They also encouraged people to study and continue learning.)*

4. **C. Defense against invasions** *(The Qin Dynasty's first emperor ordered his people to build a wall around the city to protect it from a group of barbarians called Xiongnu. It took about 2300 years and over nine dynasties to finish building the wall, which became known as the Great Wall of China, one of the seven world wonders.)*

5. **C. Buddhism** *(Buddhism is an ancient Indian philosophy and religious belief that many people still practice. Siddhartha Gautama, or Buddha, founded this faith over 2500 years ago. It has between 500 million and one billion scholars and followers. For many, it is more of a philosophy than a religion because it doesn't involve worshiping a god. The people who follow Buddhism are called Buddhists.)*

6. **D. They didn't believe in any religion** *(The Qin Dynasty emperor banned all religious and philosophical beliefs except Legalism. However, many people practiced ancestor worship.)*

7. **A. Three** *(The emperor, his wife, his family, the nobles, and some officials were on top; then farmers, peasants, laborers, and lastly the artisans and craftsmen).*

8. **B. Xin Dynasty** *(A government official named Wang Mang took advantage of the chaos that took place during the Western Han Dynasty and created a new one. However, the peasants rebelled against him, and he was killed. One of Liu Bang's descendants (named Liu Xiu) took control of the situation and started a new dynasty called Eastern Han.)*

9. **B. By Buddhist monks traveling from India** *(Buddhism arrived in China through the Silk Road, which helped spread Buddha's teachings)*

10. **A. They had knowledge of Confucius's work** *(Confucianism was the main philosophy during the Han Dynasty. The government believed that those who had knowledge of Confucius and his work had ethics and morals and were fit to serve the country. Confucius' followers also applied his five virtues, which were necessary qualities for any government official.)*

Fill in the Blanks Answers

1. **Shi Huangdi** *(Shi Huangdi's real name was Ying Zheng, and he was the founder of the Qin Dynasty. He was Qin's king and fought the other states during the Warring States period. Shi defeated the other six states, united them under his rule, and created the Qin Dynasty).*

2. **Merchants** *(They were the lowest social class, and no one respected them. Even though they were rich, they were extremely disliked because they made money off goods other people made.)*

3. **The Imperial Examination System** *(Han's emperor realized that China was so big, and he couldn't govern it alone. He hired government administrators and educated ministers to help him improve the empire, strengthen it, and keep it organized. These people were called civil servants, and they worked all over the country. Two of them were ministers and reported directly to the emperor. Thousands of civil servants played different roles in the government, such as judges, teachers, and tax collectors.)*

4. **The Han Dynasty** *(The Han emperor sent one of his men, Zhang Qian, on a diplomatic trip to the West. Zhang met many people from different cultures and civilizations on his journey. He noticed some of them had large and fast horses, unlike anything he had ever seen before. When Zhang returned to China, he told the emperor about the horses. The emperor decided to import them from the West. The horses proved to be efficient in battle, which encouraged the emperor to start trading with Europe, leading to the opening of the Silk Road.)*

5. **The people revolted** *(The people weren't happy under the Qin Dynasty's rule. The first emperor made their lives very hard. They rebelled against him and overthrew the Qin Dynasty.)*

6. **Non-hereditary bureaucratic** *(According to the Qin Dynasty's laws, no one is allowed to pass down their high position to their children or other family members. For instance, if a man was the king's minister and he died, his children wouldn't inherit his position.)*

7. **Confucianism** *(The Han Dynasty government followed Confucius's teachings, which included good morals and living in harmony with others. Emperors used his philosophy to guide them to be better rulers. If the emperors and the people followed Confucius's philosophy, everyone would live in peace, and the empire would grow and thrive.)*

8. **First emperor** *(Shi Huangdi is a title, not a name, and it means "First Emperor." Ying Zheng was the first man to unify China and rule over the whole country, making him its first emperor.)*

9. **Wang Mang** *(He was the Xin Dynasty's ruler and founder. He overthrew the Han Dynasty and ruled the country until the Han Dynasty rose back to power.)*

10. **China to Europe** *(The Silk Road connected the country with the rest of the world and allowed international trade.)*

Short Answers

1. **The magnetic compass, clepsydra, and sundial** *(The Han Dynasty was advanced, and many important inventions were made during this time, such as the compass that helped sailors find direction in the sea, the clepsydra to measure time, and the sundial which is similar to the clock and can help you tell time.)*

2. **Earthquakes** *(A seismograph detects earthquakes which sometimes occur in remote areas in ancient China.).*

3. **Shi Huangdi was paranoid** *(Shi Huangdi was always worried about death, and the situation got worse after three people tried to kill him on different occasions. He always had his sword with him and slept in a different room every night. He was so afraid of death that he became obsessed with immortality. Ironically, he died on a trip while looking for the elixir of life (a potion that would make a person immortal.))*

4. **Fear** *(He believed that some books contained false information and should be destroyed. He burned history books because he was afraid people would read them and think he wasn't a legitimate king.)*

5. **Shi Huangdi rejected Confucianism because it criticized his politics** *(The Qin Dynasty followed Legalism and reinforced strict laws that took away people's rights to speak up against his tyranny. He burned Confucius's books and killed his scholars to erase him from history. Luckily, some of Confucius's loyal followers hid his books, and his philosophy was revived during the Han Dynasty).*

6. **The Han Dynasty stands out from other ancient Chinese Dynasties for different reasons** *(It was the first dynasty to be founded by a peasant; it witnessed the invention of paper, which changed the world and brought scientific inventions that were ahead of time.)*

7. **Preventing illiteracy** *(The invention of paper helped spread literature such as poetry or stories and made books cheaper and more convenient. This gave people a chance to read and learn to prevent illiteracy.)*

8. **Han Wudi** *(He was the seventh emperor of the Han Dynasty and ruled for 54 years.)*

9. **People will find peace, joy, and all other positive feelings if they look inside themselves** *(Money, clothes, and other materialistic things won't make a person happy. Everything one needs is inside of them.)*

10. **Silk, copperwork, salt, and iron** *(China introduced silk to the world.)*

Picture-Based Query Answers

1. **The Qin Dynasty** *(The army of Terracotta soldiers helped historians learn about the Qin Dynasty, their military, and weapons. It also gave them an idea of their beliefs in the afterlife and their obsession with immortality.)*

2. **Terracotta Warriors chariot from the Qin Dynasty** *(There are no historical records of the Terracotta Warriors, and no one can say for sure if they existed or not.)*

3. **Shi Huangdi, from the Qin Dynasty** (He believed in the afterlife and chose one of his palaces as *his tomb. He ordered his artisans to create 8,000 Terracotta warriors to protect him in the afterlife. Interestingly, each one has a different face.)*

4. **The Great Wall of China from the Qin Dynasty** *(According to legend, one of the wall builders' wives went to visit her husband near the wall. However, she was told that he died. She cried so hard that part of the wall collapsed.)*

5. **Liu Bang of the Han Dynasty** *(He was one of the greatest rulers in China's history, and he cared about his people).*

6. **Buddha,** *"In the end, only three things matter: how much you loved, how gently you lived, and how gracefully you let go of things not meant for you."*

7. **The Han Dynasty** *(The Han Dynasty was famous for its art and literature.)*

8. **Eastern Han Dynasty** *(She is also called Xiwangmu, and she was one of the most important female goddesses in Chinese mythology.)*

9. **A watchtower from the Eastern Han Dynasty** *(Watchtowers are the Great Wall of China's most common features and are scattered across the wall.)*

10. **Western Han Dynasty** *(The Western Dynasty ended after the Xin Dynasty overthrew it.)*

Chapter 4: Silk, Poetry, and Porcelain: The Tang and Song Dynasties

The Tang Dynasty is one of the most influential and greatest dynasties in imperial China's history. China prospered culturally and politically during this time and became the most advanced country in the world. However, it had an unfortunate end, which paved the way for the Song Dynasty.

The Song Dynasty made many scientific and technological advancements in China. Its military was one of the most powerful worldwide, and it used new inventions to give it an advantage in battle. People were happy, and the country was growing and enjoying a time of peace and prosperity.

There is so much you can learn about these dynasties, so challenge yourself with these fun questions!

True or False

1. China's greatest inventions took place during the Tang Dynasty.

- True
- False

2. The Han Dynasty was followed by the Tang Dynasty.

- True
- False

3. The Sui Dynasty fell because its emperor died young.

- True
- False

4. The Song Dynasty is renowned for its development of blue and white porcelain.

- True
- False

5. Women weren't allowed to have an education during the Tang Dynasty.

- True
- False

6. The Song Dynasty ignored the arts and only focused on developing weapons.

- True
- False

7. Poetry was part of the civil service exam during the Song dynasty.

- True
- False

8. The Tang Dynasty produced over 50,000 literary works.

- True
- False

9. Emperor Xuanzong broke the Mandate of Heaven.

- True
- False

10. People were hired in the Tang Dynasty based on their merit, not family connections.

- True
- False

Multiple Choice

1. What changes did Emperor Taizong make?

    A. Military and government changes

    B. Education and religious changes

    C. Social changes

    D. All of the above

2. Which dynasty reunited China after the Han Dynasty fell?

    A. The Tang Dynasty

    B. The Song Dynasty

    C. The Sui Dynasty

    D. The Wei Dynasty

3. What was the name of the Song Dynasty's first emperor?

    A. Zhao Kuangyin

    B. Zhao Wun

    C. Zhao of Song

    D. Wun of Song

4. How long did the Song Dynasty rule China?

    A. 200 years

    B. 300 years

    C. 400 years

    D. 500 years

5. What was the first army in the world to use gunpowder?

    A. The Tang Dynasty

    B. The Song Dynasty

    C. The Wei Dynasty

    D. The Sui Dynasty

6. Who was on top of the Tang Dynasty's social class?

    A. Artists

    B. Buddha priests

    C. Traders

    D. The emperor and his family

7. What was the Song Dynasty's capital?

    A. Liangsu

    B. Feng Xu

    C. Bhajirag

    D. Bianjing

8. How long did it take Emperor Taizu to conquer China?

    A. 12 years

    B. 16 years

    C. 26 years

    D. 35 years

9. What was the Tang Dynasty's main religion?

    A. Taoism

    B. Confucianism

    C. Buddhism

    D. Christianity

10. Which animal did the people in the Song Dynasty use to travel?

    A. Horse

    B. Dragon

    C. Camel

    D. Wolves

Fill in the Blanks

1. _____ was the Tang Dynasty's second emperor who helped the country thrive and prosper.

2. The Tang Dynasty was the golden age of _____ and _____.

3. _____ was the Song Dynasty's biggest achievement.

4. The Tang Dynasty's capital, known for its cultural diversity and artistic vibrancy, was _____.

5. One key feature of Song Dynasty landscape paintings is _____.

6. Wu Zetian changed the name of the Tang Dynasty to _____.

7. Song's Dynasty architecture is famous for its _____.

8. The Tang Dynasty used white clay to create _____.

9. The Song dynasty was popular for its _____ paintings.

10. _____ philosophy was revived during the Song Dynasty.

Short Answers

1. She was beautiful

   She was strong

   She was an empress

   Who did no wrong

   Name this Chinese empress from the Tang dynasty.

   _____

   _____

   _____

2. Three emperors stand on a mountain high

   Making history and changing the world

   The gods watch them and sigh.

   Chanting, "*Oh, you great men are making us proud!*"

   Name the three Tang emperors who made it one of the greatest dynasties.

   _____

   _____

   _____

3. She was a powerful warrior.

   Forever a war hero;

   She conquered her enemies with her sword.

   Forever, her story will be told.

   Name the Disney princess whose story was inspired by a legend from the Tang Dynasty.

   _____

   _____

   _____

4. Made of paper, but its value is high.

   People use it for everything they buy.

   Everyone is happy to have it,

   And sad when they lose it!

   Did this invention make trading easier or more difficult?

   _____

   _____

   _____

5. Smart and clever the Tang Dynasty was,

   Its inventions were many,

   They didn't just write prose,

   The differences they made were plenty!

   Name some of the inventions from the Tang Dynasty.

   _____

   _____

   _____

6. Xuanzong was once a good king.

   All the joys to his country he would bring.

   One day, he made a mistake.

   Slowly, everything would break!

   Guess the decision Emperor Xuanzong made that brought the Tang dynasty's downfall.

   _____

   _____

   _____

7. I'll tell you a secret, but swear you won't tell.

   Revealing a secret takes you to hell,

   But some secrets get revealed,

   And make everyone pleased.

What invention did the ancient Chinese keep a secret?

_____

_____

_____

8. It was more than a piece of cloth,
   Everyone loved it for it was soft;
   The popular road was named after it.
   Can you guess what it was?

_____

_____

_____

9. More than just words that rhyme,
   I am like a painting or a song.
   I make your heart warm inside.
   What am I?

_____

_____

_____

10. Every song must end;
    It always makes people sad.
    With every end comes a beginning,
    With something new and exciting.
    Name the man who conquered China and ended the Song Dynasty.

_____

_____

_____

Picture-Based Query

1. Name this famous figure and tell me which dynasty this statue is from.

Illustration 31

Response: _____.

2. Identify this text and which dynasty it is associated with.

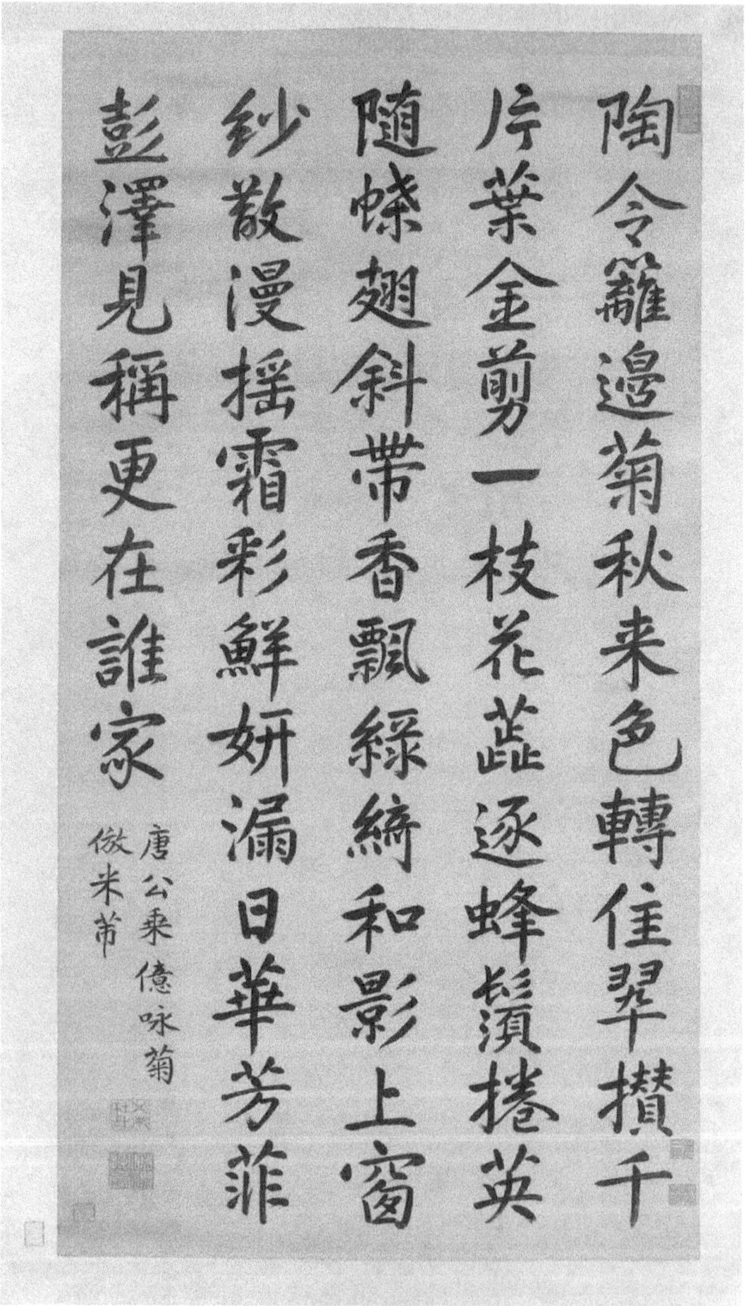

陶令籬邊菊秋來色轉佳翠攢千

片葉金剪一枝花蕊逐蜂鬚滴捲英

隨蛺翅斜帶香飄綠綺和影上窗

紗散漫搖霜彩鮮妍漏日華芳菲

彭澤見稱更在誰家

唐公乘億詠菊

倣米芾

Illustration 32

Response: _____.

3. What is this lampstand made of, and which dynasty is it from?

Illustration 33

Response: _____.

4. Identify this art style and which dynasty it is from.

Illustration 34

Response: _____.

5. Identify this art style and which dynasty it belongs to.

Illustration 35

Response: _____.

6. Identify this image and which dynasty it belongs to.

Illustration 36

Response: _____.

7. Name this famous empress, which dynasty she is from, and identify the art style.

Illustration 37

Response: _____.

8. Which dynasty does this sculpture come from?

Illustration 38

Response: _____.

9. Identify this image and the dynasty it is associated with.

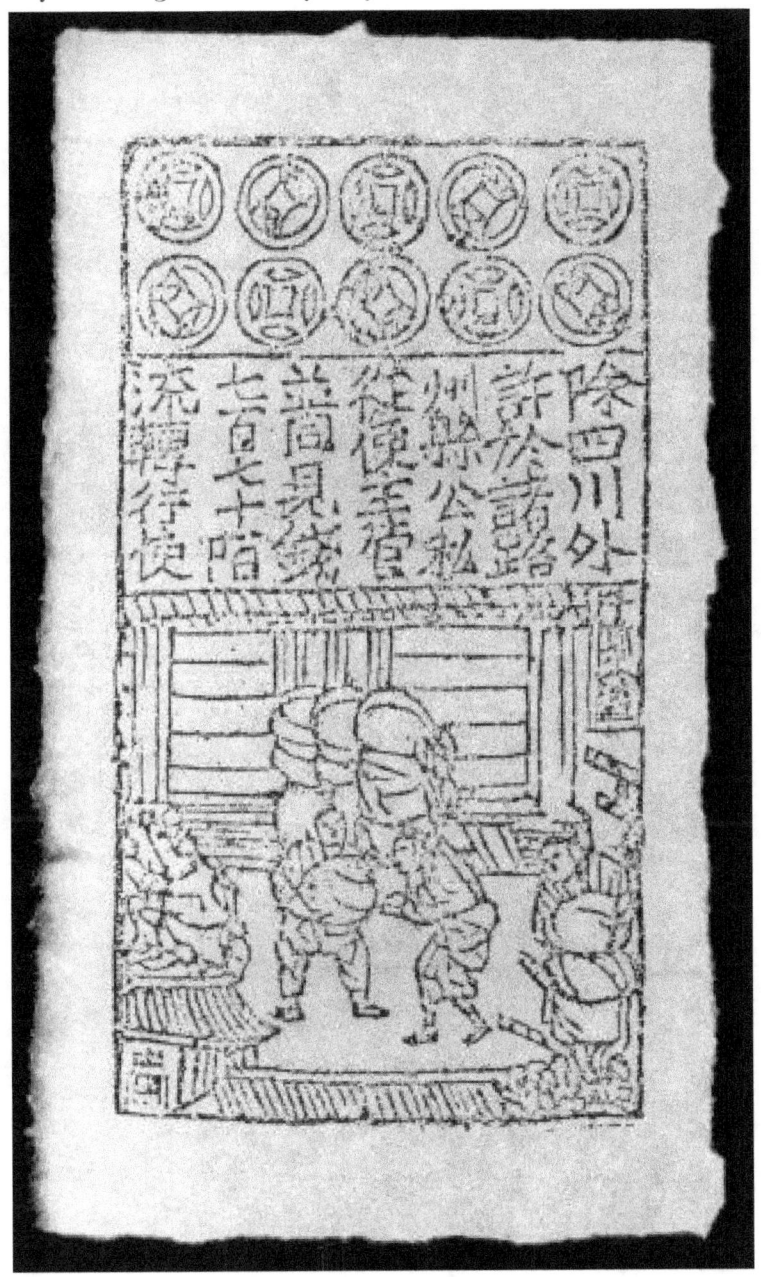

Illustration 39

Response: _____.

10. What is this artifact made of, and to which dynasty does it belong?

Illustration 40

Response: _____.

Answer Key

1. **True** *(China revolutionized the world during the Tang Dynasty with inventions in literature, architecture, technology, science, and medicine.)*

2. **False** *(After the Han Dynasty collapsed, China went through different dynasties; the Wei, Jin, Wu Hu, and Sui dynasties came before the Tang Dynasty.)*

3. **False** *(The Sui Dynasty fell because its emperor was corrupt and put his interests before his people's needs. However, things were good at the beginning, and China was advancing in many areas, including the arts. The Sui Dynasty grew more powerful, which resulted in its rulers becoming greedy. Its last two emperors only focused on expanding the military because they wanted more power and building monuments for themselves, which put the country in huge debt and led to the dynasty's downfall.)*

4. **True** *(The Song Dynasty produced blue and white porcelain in Zhejiang Province. The blue ones were very popular during the Tang dynasty. The beautiful color made it distinctive and was a great addition to many arts and crafts).*

5. **False** *(Education developed during the Tang dynasty, and men and women were allowed to go to school and learn. Historians found many famous male and female poets from the Tang dynasty, which shows that there was some equality between genders during that time. However, like many ancient cultures, women were still treated less than men in other areas.)*

6. **False** *(Art and literature advanced during the Song dynasty. The rich enjoyed painting and writing poetry during their free time.)*

7. **True** *(Poetry was a big part of the Tang and Song dynasties, which is why civil service exams tested students' knowledge of poetry. Emperor Taizong of the Tang dynasty believed that literature helped guide people and improve their manners.)*

8. **True** *(Emperor Taizong was interested in literature. He believed it was the source of wisdom. He encouraged schools to teach different types of arts, which led many to the production of thousands of works.)*

9. **True** *(Xuanzong was a just and great emperor for the first few years of his rule. However, similar to many emperors before him, he eventually neglected the country and only focused on his needs.)*

10. **True** *(The Tang dynasty only hired talented government officials. They took the civil service exams and were assigned jobs based on their scores. One's family connections and wealth weren't important. The government also opened schools so people of all classes could get an education.)*

Multiple Choice Answers

1. **D. All of the above** *(Emperor Taizong was a powerful leader. Once he took control, no one could challenge him. He gave Chinese people the freedom to practice any religion they wanted, such as Taoism, Confucianism, Buddhism, and Christianity).*

2. **C. The Sui Dynasty** *(China was divided into Northern and Southern dynasties until Sui emperor Yang Jian conquered the South and reunited the country.)*

3. **A. Zhao Kuangyin** *(The emperor was also called Taizu of Song. He was a military general and the Song dynasty's founder and first emperor. China was stable under his rule and thrived economically.)*

4. **B. 300 years** *(China prospered during the 300 years under the Song dynasty's rule.)*

5. **B. The Song Dynasty** *(The Song Dynasty made many inventions, but none was as important as the invention of gunpowder. It helped them make different weapons such as fire arrows, rickets, and bombs.)*

6. **D. The emperor and his family** *(The emperor and his family were on top of the Tang dynasty's social structure, then the aristocracy, the bureaucracy, the emperor's servants, the clergy, the peasants, and the artisans.)*

7. **D. Bianjing** *(Bianjing was one of the largest cities in the world and an economic and cultural center that was famous for trading, new inventions, and city life.)*

8. **B. 16 years** *(Emperor Taizu spent 16 years conquering and reuniting the Chinese states that were divided during the Han and Tang dynasties.)*

9. **A. Taoism** *(At the beginning of the Tang Dynasty, all religious beliefs were tolerated. However, when Xuanzong became emperor, he didn't allow his people to follow Buddhism and made Taoism the dynasty's only religion.)*

10. **C. Camels** *(Merchants used camels to transport goods across deserts. Camels can travel long distances and survive days without water.)*

Fill in the Blanks Answers

1. **Emperor Taizong** *(He was a great ruler and set a high standard for those who came after him. He became a legendary hero, and the Tang Dynasty's last good emperor, Xuanzong II, followed in his footsteps.)*

2. **Arts and culture** *(Artists explored new styles, techniques, and materials during the Tang dynasty, such as using ceramics and brushwork and experimenting with different colors. Many Tang artists were followers of Confucianism and literary scholars.)*

3. **Using paper money** *(In the seventh century, the Tang dynasty introduced private bills. In the tenth century, the Song dynasty introduced promissory notes to make up for copper coins shortage.)*

4. **Chang'an** *(Chang'an was China's greatest city and home to three million people, making it one of the most populated cities in Asia. It was located near the Silk Road and housed two of the biggest marketplaces in the country, trading everything from spices to furniture).*

5. **Attention to detail** *(The Song Dynasty's paintings had multiple other key characteristics such as poetic expressions, realism, focus on nature, and exploring different themes such as birds, flowers, landscapes, and gentlewomen.)*

6. **Zhou** *(Wu Zetian believed that she descended from the Zhou dynasty. When she became an empress, she changed Tang's name.)*

7. **Buddhist pagodas** *(The Buddhist pagodas were among the most unique and distinguished structures in ancient China. They were multi-story and tall towers that were built of stone and acted as tombs and homes for Buddhist relics.)*

8. **Porcelain** *(Porcelain allowed ancient Chinese to show their talent and creativity. It was exported worldwide during the Tang Dynasty, promoting cultural exchange and growing the country's economy.)*

9. **Landscape** *(Artists often escape to the natural world and visit places such as mountains to communicate with nature and create beautiful paintings. These paintings reflected their desire to leave everything behind and enjoy nature's peacefulness. They also showed the artists' social, political, and philosophical views.)*

10. **Confucianism** *(The Song Dynasty revived Confucianism and called it Neo-Confucianism. The new philosophy encouraged the development of one's thoughts and emotions so society could live in peace and harmony.)*

Short Answers

1. **Wu Zetian** *(She was more than just a beautiful woman; Wu Zetian improved agriculture, taxation, and education.)*

2. **Taizong, Wu Zetian, and Xuanzong** *(They were Tang's greatest emperors, and the reason China prospered for centuries.)*

3. **Mulan** *(The Disney cartoon was taken from an ancient Chinese legend that is associated with the Tang Dynasty. It is about a young girl who took her father's place in the army and became a war heroine.)*

4. **Easier** *(Carrying thousands of coins for long distances was hard on merchants. Paper money made trading much easier as it was much lighter and easy to use).*

5. **Printing, gas stoves, air conditioning, and gunpowder** *(There were many other inventions during this time, but these were the ones that made the greatest impact.)*

6. **Xuanzong** *(Xuanzong was a good and fair emperor until he made a man called Li-Linfu his chancellor. He was corrupt and selfish and planned to overthrow Xuanzong. The Tang dynasty began its downfall from that day.)*

7. **The invention of paper** *(The ancient Chinese kept the invention of paper a secret from other countries. Even the ones who saw it had no idea how it was made, and China refused to share the secret with anyone. However, it wasn't hidden for long. When the Muslims invaded China, they captured many soldiers, including paper-making craftsmen. These men had no choice but to reveal*

the secret of paper to save their lives.)

8. **Silk** *(Silk was used for clothes and paintings, and Ancient China became its main producer during the Song dynasty.)*

9. **Poetry** *(Li Bai was Tang Dynasty's most famous poet.)*

10. **Khubilai Khan** *(The Mongols invaded China and ended the Song dynasty.)*

Picture-Based Query

1. **Buddha from the Tang Dynasty** *(Buddhism is different from other religions because it focuses on people's potential and experience.)*

2. **A poem from the Tang Dynasty** *(Some of ancient China's main themes include history, politics, solitude, friendship, and life's beauty.)*

3. **White porcelain from the Tang Dynasty** *(Chinese porcelain is called china.)*

4. **Silk painting from the Tang Dynasty** *(Silk painting is popular in Vietnam, Japan, and China.)*

5. **Glazed porcelain from the Tang Dynasty** *(Glazed porcelain is highly durable).*

6. **Pottery military figures from the Song Dynasty** *(The Song Dynasty's military wasn't as strong as the Han and Tang Dynasties armies.)*

7. **Empress Xiang from the Song Dynasty, silk painting** *(She was married to Emperor Shenzong of Song).*

8. **Tang Dynasty** *(The Tang Dynasty expanded into Central Asia.)*

9. **Paper money from the Song Dynasty** *(Paper money failed in the Qing Dynasty when they kept printing more of it, and it lost its value).*

10. **Porcelain pillow from the Song Dynasty** *(In ancient China, porcelain was marked with the emperor's dynasty and reign.)*

Chapter 5: The Yuan Dynasty

The Yuan dynasty ruled China from 1271 to 1368 CE. Although their rule was short, they achieved so much during this time. The Empire enjoyed a period of peace, stability, and economic growth under the Yuan rule. The Yuan Dynasty came after overthrowing the Song Dynasty. However, conquering the Song Dynasty's armies wasn't easy. Kublai Khan and his men attacked them multiple times before they were finally defeated.

This chapter presents fun trivia questions about the Yuan dynasty to discover its journey from its rise to fall.

True or False

1. The Yuan dynasty ended because of its corrupt government, which resulted in a rebellion among the peasants.

   - True
   - False

2. The Mongols were nomadic people.

   - True
   - False

3. The Mongols weren't the first foreign people to rule China.

   - True
   - False

4. The Yuan Dynasty prospered after Kublai Khan died.

- True
- False

5. Kublai Khan allowed freedom of religion.

- True
- False

6. Genghis Khan was Kublai Khan's father.

- True
- False

Multiple Choice

1. Which country did Emperor Kublai Khan and his army attack twice?

    A. England

    B. France

    C. Japan

    D. Spain

2. Which dynasty conquered the Yuan dynasty and took its place?

    A. The Ming Dynasty

    B. The Qing Dynasty

    C. The Western Jin Dynasty

    D. None. The Yuan was the last dynasty in ancient China

3. Why did it take years for the Yuan Dynasty to conquer the Song Dynasty?

    A. The Yuan soldiers were always drunk

    B. The Yuan army leader was a traitor

    C. The Yuan army didn't have good weapons

    D. The Song army had powerful weapons

4. Which famous explorer did Kublai Khan make his diplomat?

    A. Vasco da Gama

    B. Marco Polo

    C. Francis Drake

    D. Henry Hudson

5. What was the capital of the Yuan Dynasty?

    A. Khanbaliq

    B. Xanadu

    C. Yuan

    D. A and B

6. What does "Yuan" mean?

    A. Starry Night

    B. King of China

    C. Origin of the universe

    D. Powerful gods

Fill in the Blanks

1. _____ were the rulers of the Yuan Dynasty.

2. _____ was an important trading city during the Yuan Dynasty.

3. The _____ drama was popular during the Yuan Dynasty.

4. The Yuan Dynasty's official banknote was called _____.

5. _____ painting was popular during the Yuan Dynasty.

6. Kublai Khan gave the Mongols government's _____.

Short Answers

1. How did the Yuan Dynasty treat the Mongols?

_____

_____

_____

2. How did the Mongols treat artisans?

_____

_____

_____

3. How did Genghis Khan die?

_____

_____

_____

4. What natural disasters affected China's countryside and contributed to the Yuan Dynasty's downfall?

_____

_____

_____

5. How did trading with other countries impact China's industry?

_____

_____

_____

6. Follow Marco Polo's journey and explore where he went while he was working at Kublai Khan's court.

_____

_____

_____

Picture-Based Query

1. Identify this image and what it represents.

Illustration 41

Response: _____

2. Name this important figure and mention one of his achievements.

Illustration 42

Response: _____

3. Name this figure and mention one fact about him.

Illustration 43

Response: _____.

4. What dynasty is this statue from?

Illustration 44

Response: _____.

5. Identify this image.

Illustration 45

Response: _____.

6. What religion does this statue belong to?

Illustration 46

Response: _____.

7. Identify this image and mention what it's made of.

Illustration 47

Response: _____.

8. Identify this image and mention what dynasty it's associated with.

Illustration 48

Response: _____.

9. Who does this emblem represent?

Illustration 49

Response: _____.

10. What is this artifact made of?

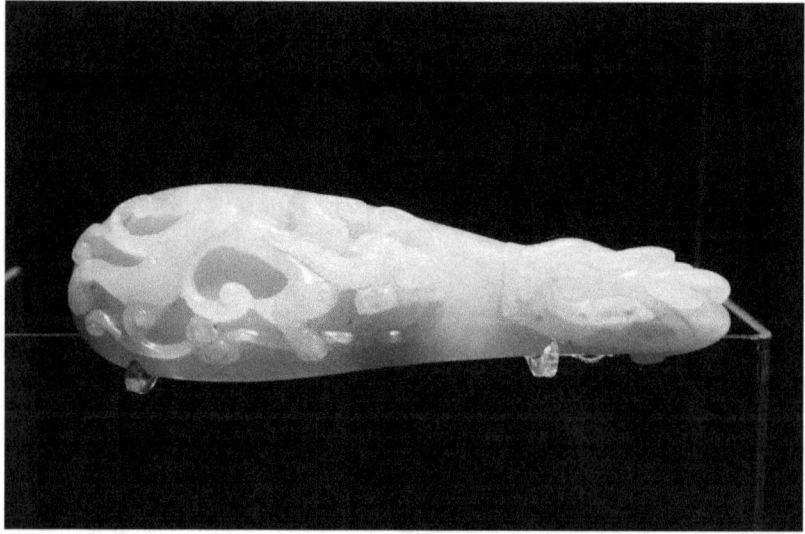

Illustration 50

Response: _____.

11. Identify key regions controlled by the Yuan Dynasty and discuss one significant trade route.

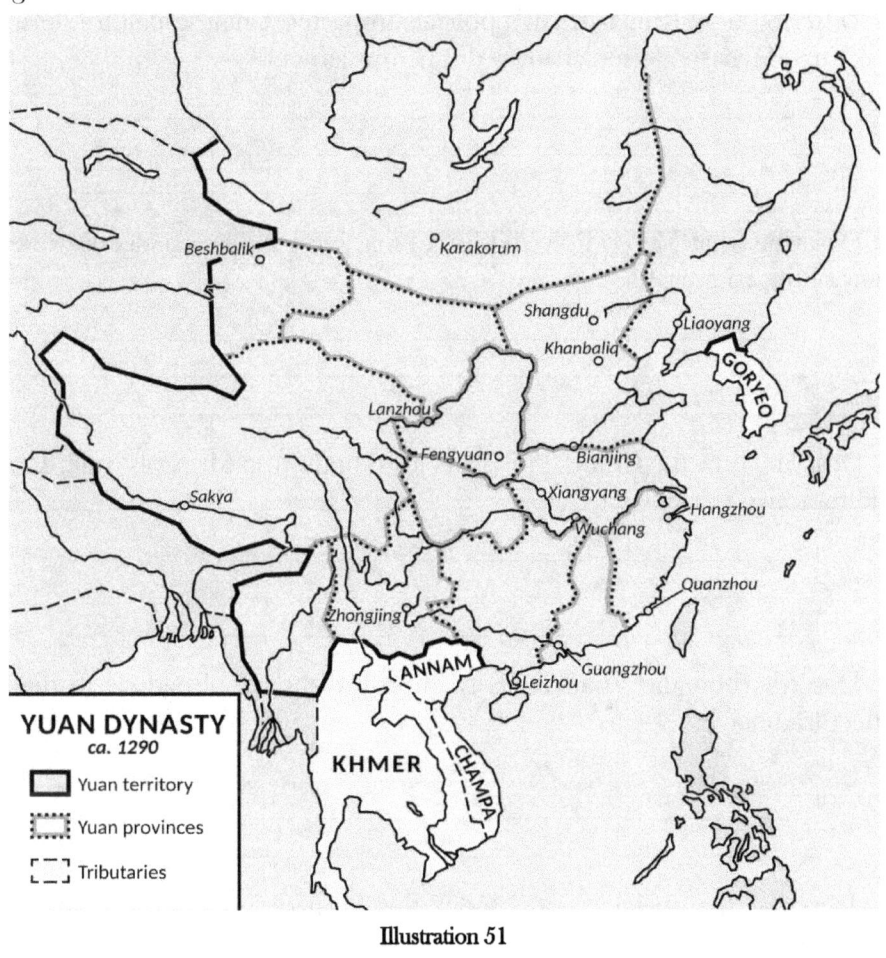

Illustration 51

Response: _____.

Cultural Crossroads

1. Describe how Kublai Khan's policies impacted Chinese culture during the Yuan Dynasty. What changes did he implement?

_____

_____

_____

2. Describe what Marco Polo did for China. How did he change Europe's view of the country?

_____

_____

_____

3. Describe how the Chinese peasants lived under the Mongols' rule. How did their lives change?

_____

_____

_____

4. Describe how the Yuan Dynasty improved the Silk Road. How did it affect trading?

_____

_____

_____

5. Describe the social classes under the Mongols' rule. How did they impact China?

_____

_____

_____

Historical Consequence

1. What were the long-term effects of the Mongol rule on Chinese society and its neighboring regions?

_____

_____

_____

2. What were the consequences of Kublai Khan's death?

_____

_____

_____

3. Did Kublai Khan try to adapt to the Chinese way of life? What were the consequences of his actions?

_____

_____

_____

4. What were the consequences of the Yuan Dynasty attacking Japan?

_____

_____

_____

5. What was the impact of the Mongol rule on the Black Death?

_____

_____

_____

Comparative Analysis

1. Compare and contrast the administrative systems of the Yuan Dynasty with those of the preceding Song Dynasty.

_____

_____

_____

2. Compare and contrast Kublai Khan with Xuanzong from the Song Dynasty.

_____

_____

_____

3. Compare the Yuan Dynasty to the Qin and Sui dynasties and analyze why they were short-lived.

_____

_____

_____

4. Compare the economy during the Tang Dynasty to that of the Yuan Dynasty.

_____

_____

_____

5. Compare the arts during the Yuan Dynasty to those of the Song Dynasty.

_____

_____

_____

Answer Key

True or False

1. True *(The Yuan Dynasty fell due to constant fighting between its leaders, high taxes, overspending, and government corruption. These led to peasant rebellion until a movement called "Red Turban" overthrew the Yuan Dynasty and brought the Ming Dynasty.)*

2. True *(Nomads are people who move from one place to the next and don't stay in one area. The Mongols moved several times a year, depending on the season, looking for food and water. They herded camels, sheep, and goats and lived in tents.)*

3. False *(The Mongols were the first foreigners to rule the whole country, but they didn't have the experience to rule a large country like China)*

4. False *(Kublai Khan was one of China's greatest rulers whose accomplishments had a huge impact on the country. He unified China, encouraged the use of paper money, and encouraged international trading. However, after he died, his successors couldn't keep the peace between the Mongols and the Chinese, which contributed to the dynasty's downfall.)*

5. True *(Kublai Khan allowed freedom of religion. People could practice Buddhism, Confucianism, Christianity, Islam, Shamanism and Tibetan Buddhism.)*

6. False *(Genghis Khan was Kublai Khan's grandfather. They shared many similarities. Both came from the same dynasty, were great rulers, and were religiously tolerant. Genghis died before conquering all of China, but his grandson finished his job.)*

Multiple Choice

1. C. Japan *(Kublai Khan and his army attacked Japan twice, but they were defeated both times. Japan's samurai warriors were invincible and protected their country from the Yuan's army. Strong storms or kamikaze (divine winds) drowned many of the Yuan Dynasty's men and ships, which also contributed to their defeat.)*

2. A. The Ming Dynasty *(The Yuan Dynasty faced many difficulties, from floods, plagues, extreme cold winters, and hunger to economic problems and rebellions. There were many divisions* *within the country, which gave the rebels the chance to defeat and overthrow the Yuan Dynasty and found the Ming Dynasty.)*

3. **D. The Song army had powerful weapons** *(In 1268, Kublai Khan wanted to make his and his grandfather's dream come true by overthrowing the Song Dynasty and ruling China. Genghis Khan and other Mongol leaders attacked the Song Dynasty. However, the Song Dynasty had advanced weapons, many ships, one million soldiers, and great wealth. They also protected main cities with walls and used clever strategies in battle. For this reason, it took the Yuan Dynasty 11 years to overthrow the Song Dynasty.)*

4. **B. Marco Polo** *(Marco Polo was a famous Venetian explorer and merchant who worked at Kublai Khan's court. He went on many adventures to various countries worldwide and wrote about them in his book "The Travels." He described the East's customs, places, and people.)*

5. **D. A and B** *(Khanbaliq, also called Dadu of Yuan, was Yuan's winter capital. Shangdu, also called Xanadu, was its summer capital. It was famous for its waterways, gardens, and palaces. Marco Polo wrote about the city in his book and described its beauty.)*

6. **C. Origin of the universe** *(After defeating the Song Dynasty and unifying China, Kublai Khan called his dynasty "Yuan.")*

Fill in the Blanks

1. **The Mongols** *(Genghis Khan founded the Mongol Empire, and he was its first "Universal Ruler" or Great Khan. He united multiple Asian nomadic tribes and built a strong army from the Mongols by choosing the strongest and fastest men. His archers and horsemen defeated some of the strongest militaries in China, East Europe, Russia, and Iran. The Mongols became very powerful and took over Asia.)*

2. **Quanzhou** *(The city became a trading center in ancient China. It was the Silk Road's starting point and a global marine during the Yuan Dynasty.)*

3. **Zaju** *(Zaju is a type of ancient Chinese poetic musical drama. It started as a short play during the Song Dynasty but turned into a four-act dramatic play with dialogue and songs during the Yuan Dynasty.)*

4. **Chao** *(Chao, also known as ziachao, was the official banknote of the Yuan Dynasty in China.)*

5. **Landscape** *(Landscape painting became very popular among Yuan artists. Zhao Mengfu was one of the most talented and influential artists during this time. He was inspired by artists from previous dynasties.)*

6. **Top jobs** *(Although Kublai tried to adapt to Chinese traditions so they could live together in peace, he only gave top government jobs to the Mongols so they would have all the power.)*

Short Answers

1. **They were given special treatment** *(Kublai ended the civil service exams that many previous dynasties used to ensure that people get government jobs based on their skills and knowledge, not their family connections. The emperor felt that these exams favored the Chinese, who were more familiar with Confucius. The exams were brought back after Kublai's death, but the Mongols still received special treatment.)*

2. **With respect** *(The Mongols valued crafts and showed their appreciation to artisans by reducing their taxes, giving them high social status, and favoring them over other occupations.)*

3. **No one knows** *(There is a lot of mystery around Genghis Khan's life and death. Many historians still argue over his death. Some believe that he died in battle, others believe that a Chinese princess murdered him to avenge her family whom he killed, while some think that he died from malaria. No one knows where he was buried, as well. It is believed that the Mongols kept his tomb a secret, but many historians think that he was buried somewhere on Burkhan Khaldun Mountain.)*

4. **Flood and drought** *(During the late 1340s, people suffered from many disasters in the countryside, such as floods and drought. The Mongol government didn't have a plan to handle these situations and protect people's lives. The Chinese became angry, which led to rebellion movements and the dynasty's downfall.)*

5. **Exchange of ideas** *(Ideas, information, techniques, and goods moved quickly and easily between Europe and Asia. For instance, Indian Christians translated the New Testament into Mongolian language. Asia also introduced Europe to insurance, deposit banking, and using paper money to buy goods.)*

Picture-Based Query

1. **The Yuan Dynasty military banner** *(It represents the army's strength. The Yuan army was called the "Han Army" and consisted of soldiers from the Southern Song troops and Jin troops from the Jin Dynasty.)*

2. **Emperor Kublai Khan** *(Kublai Khan wasn't like his grandfather, who killed many people during his attacks. He was compassionate and even presented himself as Chinese to get close to the Chinese people, which made many Mongols angry.)*

3. **Marco Polo** *(He was imprisoned in Italy three years after he returned from China. He met a writer named Rustichello of Pisa in prison. Marco told his new friend about his famous adventures, and Rustichello wrote them down. These stories became "The Travels of Marco Polo.")*

4. **A glazed porcelain sculpture from the Yuan Dynasty** *(Porcelain has been one of the biggest Chinese exports in the world.)*

5. **Paper currency** *(During the Yuan Dynasty, paper currency reduced goods prices and taxes.)*

6. **Buddhism** *(This is a statue of Guanyin, also called Avalokiteshvara. She is the goddess of mercy.)*

7. **A cannon made of bronze** *(Bronze was extremely popular in ancient China, and people kept using it even after the Iron Age)*

8. **Brown glazed jar from the Yuan Dynasty.**

9. **The Mongols emblem** *(The symbol is also featured on Magnolia's flag. The fire represents the past, present, and future. The circle and crescent represent the sun and the moon.)*

10. **Jade belt** *(Jade was one of the most popular stones in Chinese history and was used in every dynasty.)*

11. **The map covered the key regions controlled by the Yuan Dynasty** *(This includes its two capitals, Shangdu and Khanbaliq. One of the most famous trading routes at the time was the Silk Road, which helped increase trade between China and Europe.)*

Explorer's Log

When Marco Polo was 17 years old, he traveled to China with his father and uncle. Marco admired Kublai, and the emperor respected him and enjoyed his company. Marco traveled throughout China and Asia, representing the emperor and the Yuan Dynasty. He traveled to Vietnam, Sri Lanka, Indonesia, India, and Burma and returned to Kublai to tell him about what he saw and his experience, such as the people he met, their customs, and culture. The Khan explored the world through Marco's eyes, and he learned about the rest of the world from him.

Cultural Crossroads

1. Although the Mongols had a huge impact on China, most of the changes took place under Kublai Khan's rule. He encouraged trade by fixing trading routes, which improved the economy. China's architecture and literature were thriving during the Yuan dynasty. People of different religions lived in peace under his rule. This encouraged many people from all over the world to migrate to China. The empire became a cultural center. Many Buddhist temples were built, and the number of monks increased. Buddhism is still China's main religion, which shows Kublai's powerful and lasting impact on the country.

   He implemented many changes, such as reopening the Silk Road, which connected China with the Western World. He also built a canal, which had a huge impact on trade and agriculture. The Zaju genre drama was also created during Kublai's reign, which resulted in literary masterpieces such as "The Orphan of Zhao" by Ji Junxiang. In 2010, it was adapted into a movie called, "Sacrifice" highlighting the impact the Yuan Dynasty still has on modern-day China.

   Kublai also impacted architecture. He established the Yuan Dynasty capital, Khanbaliq, which was famous for its architecture and still influences many Chinese buildings.

2. Marco Polo spent 17 years in China working in Kublai Khan's court. His book "The Travels of Marco Polo" introduced China and its culture to Europe. Many Europeans have traveled to China over the years, but Marco was the only one to document his adventure, so his experiences shaped Europeans' understanding of China. Marco's book inspired many explorers, such as Christopher Columbus, to travel and explore the world.

   Many people became fascinated with China and Asia after reading Marco's book. He provided vivid descriptions of the country's culture, wealth, and more under the Yuan Dynasty. He talked about its cities, advanced technology, and goods. At the time, Europeans thought that Asia was an uncivilized and backward place, but Marco's book changed their views, and many became interested in the East's exotic goods, such as silk and spices, which increased trade between the two countries.

3. The Mongols believed that the peasants could improve China's economy and benefit the country. As a result, the Yuan government supported them by reducing their taxes and providing storage for grain in areas that were destroyed by wars between the Chinese and the Mongols. They also prevented animals from roaming in peasants' farmlands.

    However, peasants didn't have an easy life under the Yuan Dynasty. They were treated less than the Mongols and other foreigners. They were forced to join the military, and their lands were taken from them so the emperor could give them to nobles or people who would benefit him.

4. One of Kublai Khan's biggest achievements was improving the Silk Road to make trading easier. He protected the Mongol postal system, encouraged using paper money, financed trade caravans, and built infrastructure. European merchants and explorers could travel easily along the Silk Road from Europe to East Asia. They traded many goods on the famous road, such as gunpowder, paper, silk, jewels, porcelain, and horses.

5. The Mongols divided society into four classes: the Mongols were at the top, followed by the Semu people (tribes from Central Asia), the Han people (from northern China), and Southern Chinese from the Song Dynasty. The four classes didn't receive the same treatment. The Mongols had all the power and were given special treatment. The Southern Chinese were treated differently because the Mongols didn't trust them since they were associated with the Song Dynasty.

    Each class received different legal treatment based on their status. For instance, if a Mongol and a Southern Chinese committed the same crime, the Southern Chinese would receive a harsher punishment. The Southerners and Han Chinese weren't allowed to raise eagles or dogs or own weapons.

Historical Consequences

1. The Mongol Empire was one of the most powerful and influential empires in the world. Kublai made a few decisions that helped the

country grow. Many historians agree that the Yuan Dynasty and the Mongols changed the map of the world. The Mongols began as a tribe that evolved under the rule of Genghis Khan to an empire controlling China and other parts of Asia.

Genghis Khan was the reason Mongolia became a democratic country. Although he was illiterate, Genghis Khan enforced a written language within his empire after he saw the impact of literacy and writing on the Naiman tribe. The Mongol expansion contributed to the Turkic tribe's migration, allowing them to spread their culture worldwide. The map of the world changed from the 1200s to the 1500s thanks to the Mongols. Their impact on China can't be ignored as they unified the separated countries and opened the door for trade between the East and the West. This introduced China to the world and familiarized the country with other cultures.

The Mongols may have caused many destructions, but they also brought some positive changes to the world. Europe and Asia enjoyed a century of peace. This period was called "Pax Mongolica." It resulted in the Silk Road's reopening, allowing trade between Europe and Asia. Before the Mongol invasion, China and Europe didn't know much about each other. Trade familiarized both cultures with one another and allowed for an exchange of ideas, knowledge, information, and technology.

2. Kublai Khan's death began the decline of the Yuan Dynasty. While he was alive, he controlled the whole country under one empire. However, after his death, China split into four empires, which weakened the country and made it easy for the rebels to overthrow it and for the Ming Dynasty to take its place. Kublai's successors weren't as powerful or clever as he was and failed to rule the empire.

3. After Kublai Khan became emperor, he tried to get close to Chinese people by wearing the Chinese emperor's robes, seeking advice from Confucian scholars, traveling in a Sedan chair, and adopting many other customs. However, he put Chinese people in low government positions and never gave them any power, as only the Mongols were in control. His efforts and those of other Yuan rulers were superficial, and they never saw the Chinese as equals; they were considered second-class citizens. The Chinese eventually

saw through them and stood against them, which led to the empire's downfall.

4. Japan defeated the Yuan Dynasty twice, but the invasion had multiple consequences that affected both countries. The second attack on Japan caused more destruction to the Mongols than the first one. Their ships were destroyed, more than half of their soldiers were killed, and the Mongols faced many terrible losses. Some historians argue that invading Japan destroyed the Mongols' resources.

The attacks were a turning point for Japan. The country went through two invasions and was expecting a second one, so its army remained prepared for invasion for 30 years. However, this had a huge impact on the country's economy. The soldiers weren't getting paid, and they were angry. Farmers were also struggling as agriculture was suffering.

Luckily for them, the Mongols didn't attack them again. In the 13th century, the Mongol invasion was one of the biggest events in Japan's history. The country had never participated in big wars before; it only experienced small fights that usually involved a small part of the country. The Mongol invasion exposed Japan to foreign politics.

These events led to rebellious acts, a civil war that lasted for 15 years, and the fall of the Japanese government.

5. Europe was terrified of the Mongols' invasion of neighboring countries. Their empire was expanding quickly, and their attacks were cruel and brutal. They destroyed towns and killed everyone in their way. Even though they didn't attack Europe, the Europeans were panicking. The Mongol invasions contributed to the spread of the bubonic plague or the Black Death, a deadly disease that spread from flea bites and killed about 50 million people in Europe.

Comparative Analysis

1. Kublai Khan shaped the Yuan Dynasty's government after he became emperor by taking the advice of Mongols, Tibetan Buddhists, Turkic Uighurs, Jurchens, Khitans, and Chinese to create a system that fits all the different cultures living in China. The Yuan Dynasty divided the country into 11 provinces, and each one was governed by the military and the censorate (a

powerful agency from ancient China that watched administrators to prevent corruption.)

Under the Song Dynasty, the central government controlled the districts. Administrators were assigned to another unit every three years, and government generals monitored them at all times. If they made a mistake, the general would report it to the capital without telling or warning the administrator.

2. Xuanzong and Kublai Khan came from different dynasties. The Yuan Dynasty felt more like an occupation, with the Mongols taking over and the Chinese being treated as strangers in their home country. Things were different in the Song Dynasty as the Chinese were treated based on their social class rather than their nationality.

Both emperors shared many similarities. Trading was important to them, and they improved the Silk Road to make trading easier. They were both good rulers who worked on developing the country and bettering the economy, unlike some emperors in past dynasties who only focused on their interests.

However, they were still different in many aspects. While Kublai Khan gave people the freedom to practice any religion they wanted, Xuanzong made Taoism the country's main religion.

Literature and art advanced during Xuanzong's rule. Thousands of literary works were written during the Song Dynasty, unlike the Mongols, who didn't have time for poetry or prose.

Kublai and his dynasty remained powerful until he died, while Xuanzong became focused on his needs, which weakened the empire and contributed to its downfall.

3. The Yuan, the Qin, and the Sui are three of the shortest Chinese dynasties, and one can't help but wonder what they had in common that brought them their untimely downfall. Kublai succeeded in finding a balance between the Mongols and the Chinese and creating peace and harmony throughout his reign. Many of his successors struggled to achieve this balance, which resulted in rebellion. The Yuan Dynasty could have lasted longer if they had given the Chinese the same rights as the Mongols.

The Qin Dynasty lasted only for 15 years for good reason. Its rulers were cruel and tyrants. Workers who built the Great Wall of China and the canal didn't get paid and were forced to work for only a small amount of food. History books were burned, and philosophy was against the law. People from all classes didn't feel safe and couldn't put up with the rulers' tyranny, which contributed to its downfall.

The Sui dynasty only lasted for 37 years. Attacking Korea ended in a disastrous defeat, which caused many problems in the country. The peasants were also treated terribly, which led to rebellion and the overthrow of the country.

All these dynasties ended because of the way they treated their people. Tyrant empires don't last. Sooner or later, people will speak up and say no more.

4. China's economy prospered under the Tang and Yuan Dynasties. Both focused on trade and improving the Silk Road, which allowed them to trade with many countries and boost China's economy. The Tang Dynasty also developed sea routes, which allowed merchants to use different roads to trade with more countries. The Yuan Dynasty didn't just focus on trade; they also developed the handicraft industry and agriculture, which was Kublai's main focus.

5. Art flourished during the Song and Yuan Dynasties. Landscape paintings were very popular during the Song Dynasty. Painters focused on nature and creating realistic art instead of painting something from their imagination. Chinese art didn't change much during the Yuan Dynasty. Blue and white porcelain and landscape paintings were very popular. Painting was also a form of self-expression in the Yuan Dynasty.

Chapter 6: Ming Dynasty Elegance: Voyages, Architecture, and Governance

After the Mongol empire fell, the Ming Dynasty took its place. The Ming Dynasty faced many challenges from inside and outside. However, it stood tall and overcame all the plots and enemies that tried to destroy it. The dynasty kept growing and became one of the most powerful and influential in China's history.

The Ming Dynasty suffered from the same fate as all the dynasties that came before it. Corrupted government and unhappy peasants led to rebellion and the downfall of the Ming Dynasty.

Get ready to answer interesting questions and learn more about another ancient Chinese dynasty.

True or False

1. The Forbidden City is one of the biggest achievements of the Ming Dynasty.
   - True
   - False

2. The Ming Dynasty only focused on its military and ignored literature.
- True
- False

3. Women were treated equally to men in the Ming Dynasty.
- True
- False

4. The Ming Dynasty brought back civil service exams.
- True
- False

5. The Ming Dynasty continued using paper money.
- True
- False

Multiple Choice

1. Which one became China's new capital during the Ming Dynasty?
- A. Nanjing
- B. Karakorum
- C. Khanbaliq
- D. Beijing

2. Who was called China's greatest explorer?
- A. Zheng He
- B. Marco Polo
- C. Zhau Li
- D. Yongle

3. Who was the Ming Dynasty's first ruler?
- A. Li Zicheng
- B. Shen Zhou
- C. Zhu Yuanzhang
- D. Zhu Ming

4. Who were the first Europeans to trade with ancient China?

      A. The British

      B. The French

      C. The Portuguese

      D. The Spanish

5. What was the name of the opera introduced during the Ming Dynasty?

      A. Kun Qu

      B. Zhen Hu

      C. Ming Opera

      D. Zhu Ming

Fill in the Blanks

1. _____ Porcelain was popular during the Ming Dynasty.

2. _____ was the Ming Dynasty's religion.

3. The Ming's emperor grew up in _____.

4. The Ming Dynasty created _____ to collect taxes.

5. The Ming Dynasty practiced _____ to protect China.

Short Answers

1. What was the founder of the Ming Dynasty called?

_____

_____

_____

2. Where was the Ming government located?

_____

_____

_____

3. What were the voyages Zheng He went on called?

_____

_____

_____

4. Why did the Ming's treasure voyages end?

_____

_____

_____

5. How did the Ming Dynasty protect themselves from the Mongols?

_____

_____

_____

Picture-Based Query

1. Name this famous figure.

Illustration 52

Response: _____.

2. Identify this picture and mention its purpose.

Illustration 53

Response: _____.

3. Identify this image.

Illustration 54

Response: _____.

4. Identify this picture.

Illustration 55

Response: _____.

5. Identify this picture and mention what it was used for.

Illustration 56

Response: _____.

Decision-Making Scenario

1. If you were Zheng He, how would you plan a voyage to promote the Ming Dynasty's power and establish trade relations? List three key considerations.

_____

_____

_____

2. Alagakkonara, the king of Sri Lanka, didn't welcome Zheng He when he visited him to start a trade relationship between the two countries. The king tried to destroy Zheng's ships, so the explorer kidnapped the king and brought him to China. Do you agree with what Zheng did? What would you do if you were in his place?

_____

_____

_____

3. Zheng ran into a group of pirates on one of his voyages. The pirates pretended to surrender to try to escape. Zheng figured out their plan and got into a battle with them. His soldiers killed 5000 of the pirate's men and took their leader to China to be punished. If you were an explorer and ran into pirates or people who tried to steal your ship, what would you do?

_____

_____

_____

4. If you were an architect during the Ming Dynasty, what would you build and why?

_____

_____

_____

5. If you were an emperor during the Ming Dynasty, what laws would you introduce, and which ones would you change?

_____

_____

_____

Match and Learn

1. The Yu Garden. Pan Yunduan was a governor during the Ming Dynasty. He built the garden for his father so he would relax and enjoy peaceful surroundings in his old age.	 Illustration 57
2. Bao'en Temple – A Buddhist museum built for worship.	 Illustration 58
3. Zhihua Temple. Wang Zhen, one of the most powerful dictators of the Ming Dynasty, ordered his men to construct the temple.	 Illustration 59

4. The Forbidden City. It was built as a home for Chinese emperors, their families, and their servants.	 Illustration 60
5. The Ming Tombs. 16 of the Ming Dynasty's emperors are buried in these tombs.	 Illustration 61

Cause and Effect Analysis

1. Analyze the impact of the Great Wall's reinforcements during the Ming Dynasty on China's defense against invasions.

_____

_____

_____

2. Analyze the impact of Zheng He's voyages on China and its relationship with other countries.

_____

_____

_____

3. Analyze the impact of Neo-Confucianism on the Chinese people during the Ming Dynasty.

_____

_____

_____

4. Discuss the impact of the development of printing presses on the Ming Dynasty.

_____

_____

_____

5. Discuss the impact of low temperatures that occurred during the Ming Dynasty.

_____

_____

_____

Architectural Quest

1. Describe the unique features of the Forbidden City that reflect the Ming Dynasty's architectural style and cultural significance.

_____

_____

_____

2. Discuss the unique features of the Yu Gardens and how it can bring peace and relaxation.

_____

_____

_____

3. Discuss Beijing Ming City Wall Ruins Park.

_____

_____

_____

4. Describe the unique features of the Great Wall of China and its cultural significance.

_____

_____

_____

5. Describe the unique features of the Beijing Ancient Observatory.

_____

_____

_____

Policy Debate

1. Discuss the pros and cons of the sea ban policy (Haijin) implemented during the Ming Dynasty. How did it affect China's maritime activities?

_____

_____

_____

2. Discuss the pros and cons of isolationism and how it affected ancient China.

_____

_____

_____

3. Discuss the pros and cons of the civil service examination system and how it affected ancient China.

_____

_____

_____

4. Discuss the pros and cons of the Mandate of Heaven and its impact on the Ming Dynasty.

_____

_____

_____

5. Discuss the pros and cons of the Ming Dynasty's political system.

_____
_____
_____
_____

Answer Key

True or False

1. True *(The Forbidden City was ancient China's political center for over 500 years. It was home to 24 of the Ming and Qing emperors and their families. It acted as a fortress protecting the emperor and his family with its 26-foot high wall and tall guard towers. The city has 980 buildings and 90 palaces, all of which face the south to symbolize holiness. The buildings' roofs were built with yellow tiles as the color symbolized the emperor's power.)*

2. False *(Short vernacular stories were popular during the Ming Dynasty and were written in the language of the common people. The highly educated enjoyed classical literature, which was more complicated, while shop clerks, merchants, and educated women enjoyed vernacular literature. Travel writing was another popular form of literature. It focused mainly on local geography. Chinese poet Yuan Hongdao used travel literature for self-expression and to express his frustration with Confucianism's role in politics.)*

3. False *(The Ming Dynasty was a sexist society. Women's only role was to take care of the house. They weren't allowed to get jobs or be financially independent. Women were illiterate because they were denied an education.)*

4. True *(The Ming Dynasty not only revived the civil service exams but also improved them to make them different from previous dynasties' exams. They also allowed people from different classes to take the test to prevent the upper class from controlling all civil service positions.)*

5. False *(Previous dynasties, such as the Tang and Song Dynasties, introduced paper money, which made trading easier. However, paper currency became unstable during the Ming Dynasty and was replaced with silver coins imported from Japan and Spain.)*

Multiple Choice

1. D. Beijing *(The Ming Dynasty ruler, the Yongle emperor, moved the capital from Nanjing to Beijing. Beijing remained its capital for 224 years, and it was transformed during that time.)*

2. A. Zheng He *(Zheng was a Muslim scholar who served the country during the Yongle Emperor's rule. The emperor sent him on several voyages and gave him thousands of ships for his journeys,* *which were some of the largest in the world. These voyages were peaceful, and Zeng had no intention of invading any country. However, he was prepared to use force if he or his country was disrespected.)*

3. **C. Zhu Yuanzhang** *(Zhu returned to the Mandate of Heaven to strengthen his rule. He did everything in his power to protect his throne. He punished any government official who disagreed with him and made members of his family head of government in every province.)*

4. **C. The Portuguese** *(The Ming Dynasty was stable, and agriculture advanced, which impacted international trade and improved the economy. Portuguese merchants were the first to trade with China. Trading with Portugal became a big part of the economy, and the government gave them their own trading base.)*

5. **A. Kun Qu** *(Also spelled Kunqu, it was established in Kunshan city and is one of China's oldest operas. It is famous for its beautiful melodies and dynamic structure. The opera gifted the world with classic pieces such as the Hall of Longevity and the Peony Pavilion. It is a blend of symbolic gestures, acrobatics, choreographic techniques, recitals, and songs. The opera is still performed in China, and its lead characters are usually male and female. It also features an old man and multiple comic roles.)*

Fill in the Blanks

1. **Blue and white** *(Ming artists created a variety of beautiful pottery pieces, but they were most famous for their blue and white porcelain. It was exported to many countries and inspired them to create their own. Blue and white porcelain wasn't new, and many previous dynasties had manufactured it. However, the Ming Dynasty's artists perfected it. It became a symbol of the Ming Dynasty.)*

2. **Neo-Confucianism** *(Ancient Chinese scholars began questioning everything in life during the Ming Dynasty. Wang Yangming, one of its most influential scholars, was inspired by Buddhist teachings and introduced new philosophical ideas. He believed that all people, lower and upper classes, could develop their own beliefs of what is right through self-reflection and deep thinking without the need to study Confucius' work. However, their belief of what is right was subjective.)*

3. **Poverty** *(Zhu Yuanzhang was orphaned at the age of 16. He lived in the streets begging for food and money until he joined a Buddhist monastery. A few years later, the monastery burned down during a conflict between Buddhist Red Turban rebels and the Yuan Dynasty army. Zhu joined the Red Turbans, married one of his commanders' daughters, and rose to power through the ranks.)*

4. **Census** *(China's economy suffered after the Mongol rule. Natural disasters had also caused severe damage to the country. The Ming government developed reforestation and irrigation projects and relied more on agriculture than trading. While the Song Dynasty based their tax system on commerce, the Ming Dynasty used a population census to collect a proper amount of taxes.)*

5. **Isolationism** *(China was one of the wealthiest and most powerful countries in Asia during the Ming Dynasty. Unlike previous dynasties, the Ming Dynasty had no interest in expanding their empire. It was isolated from the rest of the world to protect itself from Europe's influence.)*

Short Answer

1. **Hongwu Emperor** *(After Zhu Yuanzhang became an emperor, he took the name Hongwu, meaning "abundantly martial," and named the Dynasty Ming, meaning "bright." It is believed that Zhu chose the name Ming, which refers to the god of light his group of rebels worshiped.)*

2. **The Forbidden City** *(It is called "Zijincheng" in Chinese, which means "Purple Forbidden City." It was given this name because entrance was prohibited for most citizens. Although it was home to government offices, their employees were granted limited access. Even the royal family wasn't allowed to enter all sections. Only the emperors had access to all buildings and palaces.)*

3. **Treasure voyages** *(They were given that name because they carried China's riches to show the world its power, wealth, treasure, and prestige.)*

4. **Financial problems** *(The fleet treasures ended for various reasons. The Yongle Emperor sponsored these voyages, but after his death, things changed. His successor, the Hongxi Emperor, didn't have his father's passion and put an end to these voyages. They were also very expensive and cost the country a lot of money. They weren't trade voyages, so they didn't bring any money. The*

Hongxi Emperor realized that the country was in financial trouble due to these unnecessary adventures, so he ended them.)

5. **By strengthening the Wall of China** *(The Wall of China was neglected throughout China's history. Previous dynasties didn't pay much attention to it or maintain it. When the Ming Dynasty came to power, the wall was in bad condition. The Mongols constantly threatened the Ming Dynasty. The Ming government realized that restoring and strengthening the wall would protect them and prevent further attacks.)*

Picture-Based Query

1. **Zhu Yuanzhang** *(The founder of the Ming Dynasty accomplished many things. He built local schools and made education available for everyone, revived the civil service exams, and contributed to art by founding the Painting Academy at Nanjing.)*

2. **Bianjing Drum Tower** *(This 129-foot building contained bells and drums that were used as musical instruments, and later, the government used them to tell the time.)*

3. **Beijing Ming City Wall Ruins Park** *(The park is home to the Ming City Wall ruins, which the Ming government built to protect itself from the Mongols' attacks)*

4. **Beijing Ancient Observatory** *(It was built in 1442 and was the observatory of the Ming and Qing Dynasties. Eight of its astronomical instruments are still intact.)*

5. **Zheng He ship** *(The largest ships in Zheng's fleet were called "Baoshan" or treasure ships. They were 210 feet wide and about 440 feet long. Zheng also had smaller ships that carried horses, goods, and food for the crew. The smallest ones were designed for battle. Interestingly, the smallest ships were twice as big as Christopher Columbus's ship, the Santa Maria.)*

Match and Learn

1. **Picture 2** *(The Yu garden was one of the largest and most elegant gardens at the time. "Yu" is a Chinese word that translates to peaceful and pleasing. It has a very unique design with a zigzag bridge, sculpted rockeries, mid-lake pavilions, clay sculptures, inscriptions of past dynasties, brick carvings, and paintings and calligraphy by famous artists.)*

2. **Picture 5** *(The temple reflects the beauty of the Ming Dynasty's art with its sculptures, paintings, murals, and other ornamental additions.)*

3. **Picture 4** *(The Zhihua Temple is one of the most preserved architectural structures from the Ming Dynasty in Beijing. It is filled with beautiful designs that showcase the brilliance of the Ming Dynasty's architects and artists, such as Ten Thousand Buddha's Hall.)*

4. **Picture 1** *(It took one million workers, one hundred thousand craftsmen, and 14 years to finish constructing the Forbidden City. It is three times larger than the Louvre Castle and is home to some of the world's most preserved wooden structures. It is a testimony to the Ming Dynasty's architectural mastery. For instance, the roof was designed in a unique way to prevent birds from landing on the roof and to keep it clean.)*

5. **Picture 3** *(These tombs were built inside the Tianshou Mountain to create a collection of magnificent mausoleums. This tomb complex is the largest in the world and reflects ancient China's rich and fascinating culture. The tombs are considered a great design achievement for blending landscape art with architecture.)*

Cause and Effect Analysis

1. The Mongols kept attacking the Ming Dynasty until they succeeded in kidnapping its Emperor Zhengtong. They asked for ransom to return him, but the Ming officials decided to replace him with his half-brother instead. The Ming government realized that they needed to reconstruct the Great Wall because it was their strongest defense against the Mongols' attacks. The Great Wall of China prevented nomadic tribes such as the Mongols from entering China and causing havoc.

2. Zheng He's voyages expanded ancient China's cultural and political influence worldwide. He succeeded in establishing diplomatic ties with other countries and bringing knowledge and information about the West that fascinated the East and made them curious about other cultures. Ancient China owed so much to Zheng's expeditions as they increased China's power and influence. He showed the world China's wealth, rich culture, and civilization.

3. Neo-Confucianism played a big role in maintaining and establishing order in ancient China throughout the Ming Dynasty. Buddhist

and Taoist beliefs integrated with Confucianism, which led to an advancement in literary and artistic expressions such as poetry, painting, and calligraphy. Neo-Confucianism borrowed the same values from Confucianism and stressed the significance of morals, community, and family. These beliefs helped ancient Chinese people develop a sense of cooperation, harmony, and responsibility. Neo-Confucianism spread to other countries around Asia, which allowed for cultural and philosophical exchange.

4. The invention of the printing press lowered book prices, which made them easily accessible to all classes. This reduced illiteracy and allowed for the spread of knowledge.

5. There was a period in ancient China's history called the Little Ice Age. It refers to a period of a colder climate and glaciation that caused famine in various places around the world, including China. Many historians believe that it contributed to the downfall of the Ming Dynasty. In 1620, the temperature in ancient China severely dropped, which impacted crops. The country was also affected by other natural disasters, such as floods, drought, and famine, which weakened the Ming Dynasty.

Architect Quest

1. The Forbidden City's unique design is what makes it an architectural masterpiece and one of China's most significant monuments. Ancient Chinese believed that the emperor was the son of heaven, so his home should reflect his sacred status. The Forbidden City's main halls and gates were arranged on the north-south central axis. They believed that heaven was the north star, and the city pointed straight to it. It also has the only complete wooden structure in the world. The mainframes of the buildings were made of wooden columns and beams. However, no nails were used because they were believed to be violent.

2. The Yu Garden has unique features that showcase the Ming Dynasty's architectural achievements and also invite peacefulness and relaxation, such as beautiful rockeries, archways, pagodas, glittering pools, and decorative halls. A walk through its archways will help you forget all your stresses. The magnificent Jade Rock stands out on its long corridors.

3. Only two remaining Ming Dynasty city walls are still standing in Beijing. One extends from Chongwenmen to the southeast tower, which symbolizes the city. It is also the only remaining part from the original wall. The southeast corner tower is the largest remaining tower and was built during the reign of Emperor Zhengtong of Ming.

4. Two of the Great Wall's main architectural features are its breathtaking landscape and defensive functions. Craftsmen, military strategists, architects, and civil engineers worked together to enhance the wall's longevity and performance. Ramparts, battlements, and watchtowers were placed strategically to increase defense, communication, and surveillance. The highest-quality materials were used to build the wall and to ensure it could survive natural disasters and attacks.

5. It is one of the oldest observatories in the world and home to some of the most advanced ancient instruments. It is 58 feet high and is located in central Beijing. Astronomers used it during the Ming and Qing Dynasties to watch the stars and other celestial bodies in the sky and report their movements to the king since he was the "Son of Heaven." Although the main focus here is the instruments rather than the architecture, one can't help but admire the building's simple design and the aesthetic way the instruments are positioned.

Policy Debate

1. The Ming Dynasty rulers applied the sea ban policy during the isolationism period when they restricted sea trading and isolated China from the rest of the world. Haijin was first imposed to protect Chinese fleets against Japanese pirates. However, the ban backfired. Sailors who were affected by the sea ban turned to smuggling and piracy. Ming Dynasty emperor and founder Zhu Yuanzhang introduced this policy, which negatively impacted the country's growth and trade. Even though the policy proved to be counteractive, it lasted for a long time. The ban still had some advantages. It freed the Ming army to secure the country's borders and destroy Yuan loyalists.

2. Isolationism made trading and cultural exchange between China and other civilizations challenging. On the other hand, it protected China from invasion and allowed it to develop a unique culture

away from the West's influence.

3. The civil service exams allowed all classes to work in government positions by providing a fair system that tested people's knowledge of Confucianism, literature, and writing. People were chosen based on their achievements, not their social class and family connections. However, these exams were extremely difficult and allowed few peasants or artisans who passed to move up to the upper class.

4. The Mandate of Heaven reminded emperors that they had moral obligations toward their subjects and they should be fair, kind, and compassionate rulers who put their people's needs first. If a ruler became a tyrant or neglected his duties, the Mandate of Heaven gave people the right to overthrow him. However, some people used it as an excuse to destroy a ruler or a dynasty so they could take their place.

5. The Ming Dynasty made many achievements during their time, such as restoring the Great Wall, sending treasure voyages to showcase China's power and culture to the world, reviving civil exams, and increasing international trade and economic growth. However, they also suffered from a few setbacks, such as government overspending and corruption, which led to the rebellion of peasants.

Chapter 7: Daily Life and Society in Ancient China

Have you ever wondered what life was like for ancient Chinese people? Life was different for them back then. They didn't have the technology or comforts that many people take for granted nowadays. They also had to live under strict rules with emperors who didn't always have their people's best interests at heart. Take a trip back in time and walk in the shoes of people who lived centuries ago in a faraway land.

True or False

1. Most of the ancient Chinese were peasant farmers.

   - True
   - False

2. Ancient Chinese women could easily divorce their husbands.

   - True
   - False

3. All children went to school in ancient China.

   - True
   - False

4. Ancient Chinese respected the dead.

- True
- False

5. All people dressed the same in ancient China.

- True
- False

Multiple Choice

1. What colors were peasants allowed to wear during the Sui Dynasty?

    A. Red and green

    B. Yellow and navy

    C. White and gray

    D. Black and blue

2. What was the most popular drink in ancient China?

    A. Strawberry juice

    B. Tea

    C. Coffee

    D. All of the above

3. What was the lowest class in ancient China?

    A. Farmers

    B. Teachers

    C. Merchants

    D. Construction workers

4. What part of their body the ancient Chinese didn't cut?

    A. Hair

    B. Fingernails

    C. Toenails

    D. All of the above

5. What were criminals marked with?

    A. Piercings

    B. Short hair

    C. Black clothes

    D. Tattoos

Fill in the Blanks

1. Marriage in ancient China was arranged by _____.

2. _____ was the most popular type of art.

3. _____ means respecting one's elders in ancient China.

4. A person's social class was determined by _____.

5. _____ was the most common crop in ancient China.

Short Answers

1. What was life like for women in ancient China?

_____

_____

_____

2. Who were the only people allowed to wear silk?

_____

_____

_____

3. What did footbinding do to girls' and women's feet?

_____

_____

_____

4. What did ancient Chinese stories have in common?

_____

_____

_____

5. Why were kings called emperors?

_____

_____

_____

Picture-Based Query

1. Identify this image and mention what it was made of.

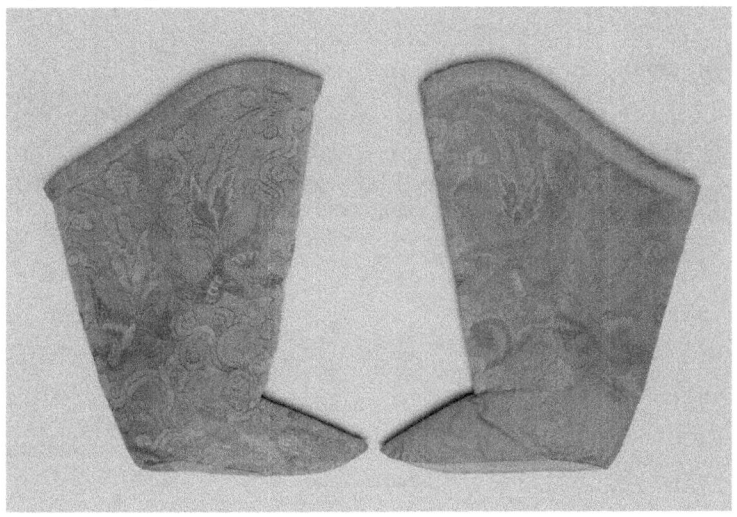

Illustration 62

Response: _____.

2. What popular ancient Chinese game is played in this picture?

Illustration 63

Response: _____.

3. Identify this image.

Illustration 64

Response: _____.

4. What event is celebrated in this image?

Illustration 65

Response: _____.

5. Describe what is going on in this picture.

Illustration 66

Response: _____.

A Day in the Life/Imaginative Role-Play

1. Imagine you are a merchant during the Tang Dynasty. Describe a typical day, including your interactions and the types of goods you might trade.

_____

_____

_____

2. Imagine you are a farmer during the Yuan Dynasty. Describe a typical day, including your interactions with other farmers and the crops you are growing. Describe your daily challenges as a peasant.

_____

_____

_____

3. Imagine you are a scholar-official from the Zhou Dynasty working with Confucius. What would you talk about? What questions would you ask him? Describe your daily interactions.

_____

_____

_____

4. Imagine you are a government official during the Qin Dynasty. What rules would you change, and which ones would you introduce to the country? Describe your daily interactions.

_____

_____

_____

5. Imagine you are a noble during the Han Dynasty. What would you do to help the peasants? Describe your daily interactions and challenges you might face while helping the poor.

_____

_____

_____

Social Structure Puzzle

Illustration 67

1. Identify the social classes in this picture from lowest to highest.

_____

_____

_____

2. Mention the social class that was allowed to wear silk and own lands and another social class that worked for them.

_____

_____

_____

3. They ruled the country, and no one´ dared question them or their families. Who were they?

_____

_____

_____

4. They were considered the lowest class and treated differently from everyone else. Who were they?

_____

_____

_____

5. What social class were the philosophers, scholars, and thinkers?

_____

_____

_____

Compare and Reflect

1. Compare your daily life with that of a child in ancient China. What are the most striking differences and similarities?

_____

_____

_____

2. Compare how girls were treated in ancient China to how they are treated today. What are the most striking differences and similarities?

_____

_____

_____

3. Compare the life of ancient Chinese and the struggles they faced due to lack of technology to how easy life is for you in the modern world. What are the most striking differences?

_____

_____

_____

4. Compare ancient Chinese rulers to presidents in modern times. How have things changed?

_____

_____

_____

5. Compare how hard it was for Chinese children to get an education to how much easier it is for you in modern times.

_____

_____

_____

Customs and Traditions

1. Describe one ancient Chinese festival and its significance in society.

_____

_____

_____

2. Describe one marriage tradition in ancient China.

_____

_____

_____

3. Describe one funeral tradition in ancient China and mention its significance.

_____

_____

_____

4. Describe how ancient Chinese greeted each other.

_____

_____

_____

5. Describe how ancient Chinese celebrated the New Year.

_____

_____

_____

Ethical Dilemmas

1. As a Confucian scholar-official, what would be your approach to resolving a local dispute? Consider Confucian principles in your answer.

_____

_____

_____

2. As a legalism scholar-official, what would you do when a poor person steals to feed their family?

_____

_____

_____

3. As a Buddhist scholar-official, what would you do if you saw someone treated unfairly?

_____

_____

_____

4. As a Taoism scholar, what would you do if a person were afraid to tell a truth that could save someone's life?

_____

_____

_____

5. As a Confucian scholar-official, what would you do if someone close to you committed a crime?

_____

_____

_____

Answer Key

True or False

1. True *(The majority of ancient Chinese were farmers. They lived in small communities and worked on farms, which, in some cases, belonged to the nobles and not to them. Peasants and farmers led hard lives and were deprived of many of the luxuries that the nobles enjoyed. They didn't even have their basic rights such as education.)*

2. False *(Women weren't allowed to divorce their husbands, but men could end the marriage for different reasons, some of which were very superficial, such as talking too much.)*

3. False *(Only older boys from rich and noble families were allowed to go to school. Poor children were denied an education).*

4. True *(Ancient Chinese respected and honored their dead and venerated their ancestors. Confucius also called for respecting the elderly and their ancestors. The way ancient Chinese buried their dead showed their respect for them. They washed and dressed them and made offerings to them, such as incense and food.)*

5. False *(Men and women dressed differently in ancient China. Women wore long tunics that went to their ankles, blouses, dresses, or skirts. Men wore short tunics with pants under them and short jackets in the winter. During the Song Dynasty, women's clothes were fastened on the left. Ancient Chinese mothers sewed an image of a tiger on their children's clothes for protection.)*

Multiple Choice

1. D. Black and Blue *(During the Sui Dynasty, the emperor passed a law prohibiting peasants from dressing like the upper class. The peasants only wore black or blue, while the wealthy wore any color they wanted.)*

2. B. Tea *(Tea was the most popular drink in ancient China among all classes. It became a favorite for Buddhist monks after they realized that the caffeine kept them awake for hours during meditation. Rice wine was another common drink in ancient China. No one knew who invented it, but it became popular during the second century.)*

3. **C. Merchants** *(Merchants were the lowest class in ancient China. Although they made more money than craftspeople and farmers, they were treated as inferiors due to their jobs. Traders didn't produce anything; they only bought and sold products, unlike farmers who produced food and artisans who created goods with their hands. Many believed that merchants were greedy and didn't deserve any respect.)*

4. **A. Hair** *(Ancient Chinese men and women from all classes didn't cut their hair because they believed it was a gift from their ancestors. They let their hair grow out of respect for them.)*

5. **D. Tattoos** *(Criminals were marked with tattoos on their faces and exiled to another region. Even if they burned off the tattoo and returned, it would leave a scar that would allow people to recognize their criminal past.)*

Fill in the Blanks

1. **Parents** *(People didn't get married in ancient China out of love. Parents arranged their children's marriage. They usually choose families based on their economic or social status. Some even chose partners for their children based on their astrological signs. The bride and groom didn't have a say, and some didn't meet until the wedding day.)*

2. **Calligraphy** *(Calligraphy was more than just a type of handwriting in ancient China; it was a type of art that was more valuable than sculptures and paintings. Calligraphy was as respected as poetry and was considered a means for self-expression.)*

3. **Filial piety** *(Confucius taught his students the concept of filial piety. It stresses the importance of loving, respecting, and supporting one's parents, grandparents, and other elderly members of one's family. A person should obey their parents, listen to their advice, and take care of them when they get old.)*

4. **Birth** *(If a person's father was a peasant, they would also be a peasant. During the Han Dynasty, people could improve their social status by taking and passing the civil service exams and working for the government.)*

5. **Rice** *(One of the things that ancient and modern China had in common was their love for rice. It has always been the country's most significant crop, and they incorporate it in many recipes.)*

Short Answers

1. **Difficult** *(Ancient Chinese women didn't have the same rights as men, whether politically or socially. Before marriage, their fathers were in control of their lives, and after marriage, the control went to their husbands. If they became widows, their sons would be responsible for their estate, and they didn't have a say in anything.)*

2. **Royalty and nobles** *(The emperor, his family, and the nobles were the only ones who wore silk. Neither the silk merchants nor the people who made it were allowed to wear it.)*

3. **Smaller** *(Foot-binding was a practice that took place during the Tang Dynasty. It was only done to little girls to keep their feet small and limit their movements. It was a permanent and extremely painful procedure. Only the upper class used to do it, but later, the lower class joined the trend, which lasted until the 20th century.)*

4. **Morals** *(Each story in ancient Chinese literature had different animals and objects that were symbols and represented something bigger and deeper. There were messages behind these characters and stories that teach readers moral lessons.)*

5. **To reflect their prestige** *(Ancient Chinese rulers began using the term "Emperor" during the Qin Dynasty. They wanted to distinguish themselves from previous kings and reflect their prestige as more powerful rulers than those who came before them).*

Picture-Based Query

1. **Shoes made of silk** *(The upper class wore soft shoes made of silk while the lower class wore sandals or boots made of straw.)*

2. **Liubo** *(It was a board game that required two players. It originated from the Warring States period.)*

3. **Ancient Chinese homes** *(Ancient Chinese homes differed depending on each person's social status. Lower classes, such as peasants and farmers, lived in huts. Middle-class people such as merchants lived in houses made of wood.)*

4. **Ancient Chinese weddings** *(If the groom died before the wedding, the ceremony would still take place, and the bride would live with his family as a widow.)*

5. Ancient Chinese funeral (*During a funeral, the body of a dead person was placed in a coffin made of an old tree trunk.*)

Social Structure Puzzle

1. Farmers, craftsmen, artists, and warriors.

2. The nobles.

3. The emperors.

4. The peasants.

5. Elite class.

Customs and Traditions

1. The Qixi Festival is one of the most interesting ancient Chinese festivals that is still celebrated on the seventh day of the seventh lunar month. It goes by many names, such as the Night of Sevens or Chinese Valentine's Day. There is a beautiful legend behind this festival that was celebrated during the Han Dynasty. A young farmer fell in love with a young woman from heaven. However, when the queen of heaven found out, she separated the two lovers. They spent years trying to get back together, and they were finally reunited that day. Ancient Chinese girls spend the day praying for a good husband. Now, it has become similar to Valentine's Day, when lovers celebrate their love. It is also a reminder of the importance of romance, and that love conquers all.

2. Most ancient Chinese wedding traditions originated from the Han Dynasty. One of the most significant traditions was the gift exchange between the groom's and bride's families and dowry. No marriage should take place without this custom. If it did, it would be considered dishonorable. After the gift exchange, the bride went to live at her groom's family home.

3. Ancient and modern Chinese, especially Buddhists, dispose of the dead by fire through a method called cremation. However, the bodies of the upper wealthy weren't cremated right away. They were kept at a temple for a year out of respect for the deceased. During this time, religious ceremonies were held in their honor, such as songs, speeches, and gifts that would benefit them in the afterlife.

4. Zuoyi is an ancient Chinese greeting from the Western Dynasty that has been around for over 3000 years. It is a fist-and-palm salute and a symbol of respect and appreciation.

5. New Year's celebration was the most significant festival in ancient China. The people welcomed this day with fireworks to drive away evil spirits. They also made sacrifices to the gods to ensure the land would be fertile in the coming year. Shops were closed, and the government would go on vacation for seven days. People spent that time expressing their gratitude for the past year and preparing for the next by making offerings to protect their homes from evil.

Chapter 8: Inventions and Discoveries: China's Contributions to the World

Although ancient China didn't have many of the inventions that you have today, they were still ahead of their time. Many of their discoveries changed history and showed how brilliant and hardworking ancient Chinese people were. This chapter focuses on China's contributions to the world with fun and creative questions.

True or False

1. Ancient Chinese used to write on silk.

   - True

   - False

2. Ancient Chinese invented toilet paper.

   - True

   - False

3. Ancient Chinese weren't the first people to invent the astronomical clock.

   - True

   - False

4. Ancient Chinese invented Calligraphy.

- True
- False

5. Ancient Chinese are described as uninventive.

- True
- False

Multiple Choice

1. Which material did the compass need to work?

A. Bronze

B. Silver

C. Jade

D. Lodestone

2. Which legendary empress invented silk?

A. Leizu

B. Li Wu

C. Wu Zetian

D. Empress Zhangsun

3. What did the Chinese write on before they invented paper?

A. Bamboo

B. Bones

C. Tortoiseshells

D. All of the above

4. What did Bi Sheng invent?

A. Paper

B. Movable type technology

C. Compass

D. Books

5. Which ancient Chinese invention was accidental?

A. Paper

B. Silk

C. Gunpowder

D. Carriages

Fill in the Blanks

1. _____ is an ancient Chinese invention that detects Earthquakes.

2. _____ is an ancient Chinese medicine that involves the use of needles.

3. _____ is a Chinese invention that can leave a person intoxicated.

4. _____ were a great agricultural invention.

5. The ancient Chinese called _____ broom stars.

Short Answers

1. What did ancient Chinese use kites for?

_____

_____

_____

2. What did the ancient Chinese use compasses for?

_____

_____

_____

3. What made woodblock printing easier and cheaper?

_____

_____

_____

4. What did the ancient Chinese discover about the human body?

_____

_____

_____

5. What did the ancient Chinese discover about the moon?

_____

_____

_____

Picture-Based Query

1. Name this ancient Chinese game.

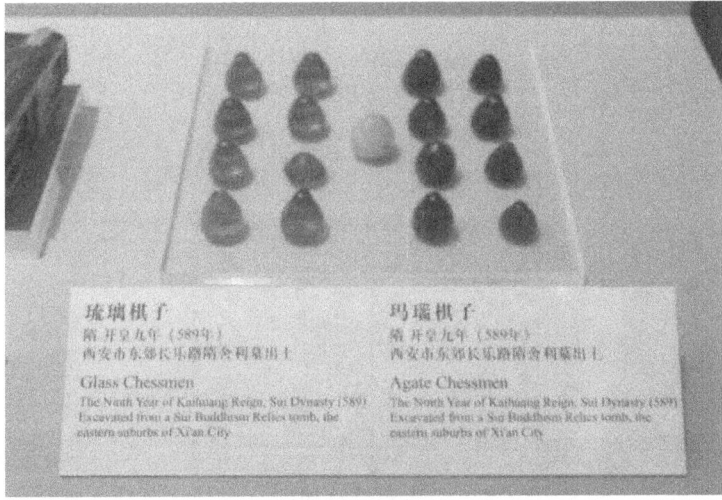

Illustration 68

Response: _____.

2. Name this ancient Chinese invention.

Illustration 69

Response: _____.

3. Name this weapon.

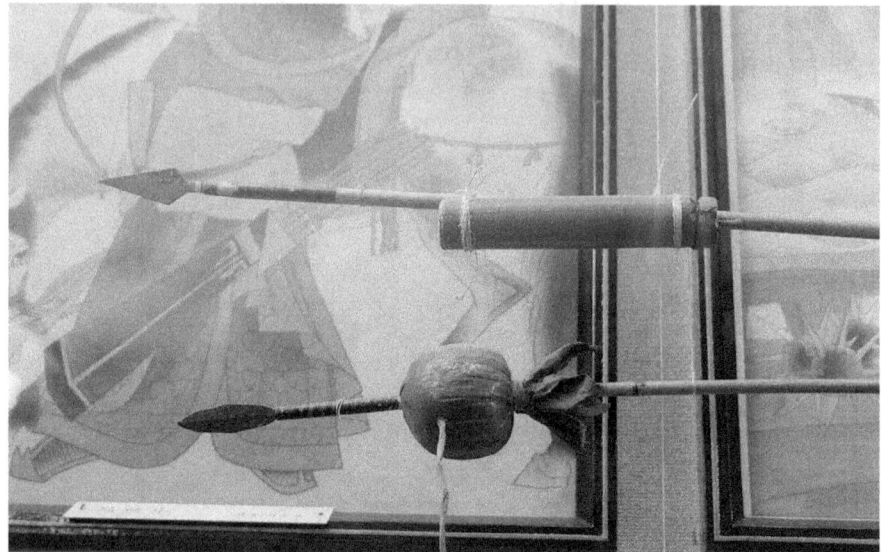

Illustration 70

Response: _____.

4. Name the person who invented the wheelbarrows.

Illustration 71

Response: _____.

5. Name the famous architect whose wife invented the umbrella.

Illustration 72

Response: _____.

Creative Improvement

1. The compass was invented in ancient China. How could you modify it with modern technology to enhance its functionality?

_____

_____

_____

2. The umbrella was invented in ancient China. What changes and improvements would you make to it?

_____

_____

_____

3. Chess was invented in ancient China. What changes and improvements would you make to it?

_____

_____

_____

4. The paper was invented in ancient China. What changes and improvements would you make to it?

_____

_____

_____

5. The wheelbarrows were invented in ancient China. How could you modify it with modern technology to enhance its functionality?

_____

_____

_____

Global Influence

1. Discuss the impact of Chinese papermaking on global knowledge dissemination and education.

_____

_____

_____

2. Discuss the impact of Chinese acupuncture on medicine.

_____

_____

_____

3. Discuss the impact of Chinese Seismographs to help save people's lives.

_____

_____

_____

4. Discuss the impact of Chinese gunpowder and if its invention was good or bad.

_____

_____

_____

5. Discuss the impact of the Chinese compass on helping sailors find directions.

_____

_____

_____

Inventor's Dilemma

1. If you were an ancient Chinese alchemist who accidentally invented gunpowder, what would be your initial intended use for it?

_____

_____

_____

2. If you were the inventor of paper in ancient China. Would you keep it a secret or share it with the rest of the world? List your reasons for choosing this option.

_____

_____

_____

3. If you invented alcohol in ancient China, what would you use it for?

_____

_____

_____

4. If you invented paper money, how would you want people to use it?

_____

_____

_____

5. If you were an ancient Chinese inventor who invented cannons, what would be your initial intended use for them?

_____

_____

_____

Technological Timeline

1. Place the following Chinese inventions in chronological order: compass, paper, gunpowder, and printing.

_____

_____

_____

2. Place the following Chinese inventions in chronological order: umbrellas, wheelbarrows, alcohol, and mechanical clocks.

_____

_____

_____

3. Place the following Chinese inventions in chronological order: tea, silk, acupuncture, and porcelain.

_____

_____

_____

4. Place the following Chinese inventions in chronological order: seismographs, rockets, bronze, and kites.

_____

_____

_____

5. Place the following Chinese inventions in chronological order: Paper money, toothbrushes, canons, and fireworks.

_____

_____

_____

Innovation Analysis

1. Analyze how the invention of silk affected both ancient China's economy and its interactions with other civilizations.

_____

_____

_____

2. Analyze how the invention of paper money affected trade in ancient China.

_____

_____

_____

3. Analyze how the invention of gunpowder affected the war against the Mongols.

_____

_____

_____

4. Analyze how the invention of paper helped ancient Chinese fight illiteracy.

_____

_____

_____

5. Analyze the impact of the invention of porcelain on Europe.

_____

_____

_____

Answer Key

True or False

1. **True** *(Ancient Chinese used to write their books on wood or bamboo. However, they were mainly drafts. They wrote the final editions on silk. Ancient Chinese had been writing on silk since the sixth or seventh century. Thanks to its size, it provided a large writing surface, which they used for formal inscriptions, maps, and illustrations.)*

2. **True** *(Toilet paper was invented in 851 A.D. during the Han Dynasty. It was made from tree bark and silk. However, only the emperors and their families were allowed to use it.)*

3. **False** *(A Buddhist monk named Yi Xing invented the astronomical clock in 725 A.D. Centuries later, an inventor from the Song Dynasty named Su Song created a more advanced clock called the Cosmic Empire. This was years before the mechanical clock was invented in Europe.)*

4. **True** *(Calligraphy was invented during the Shang Dynasty, but it became popular during the Han Dynasty among court women and educated men. It became one of the most significant art forms in ancient China.*

5. **False** *(Ancient China was one of the most inventive civilizations worldwide. They didn't only invent paper and gunpowder, which revolutionized the world, but they also made many contributions to agriculture, astronomy, and shipping, and the modern world will forever be indebted to it.)*

Multiple Choice

1. **D. Lodestone** *(Ancient Chinese used the mineral lodestone, which acted as a magnet that aligned with the Earth's magnetic field.)*

2. **A. Leizu** *(According to ancient Chinese legend, Empress Leizu, the Yellow Emperor's wife, invented silk around 2696 or 2700 B.C. One day, the young empress was having tea in her garden. Suddenly, a cocoon fell into her cup. It caught her attention, and she examined it. She noticed that it was made from soft and long threads. She learned how to combine the silk fibers and turn them into soft fabric. It is believed that she also invented the silk loom. The empress came to be known as the goddess of silk.)*

3. **D. All of the above** *(Before the invention of paper, the ancient Chinese used to write on tortoise shells, animal bones, and bamboo.)*

4. **B. Movable type printing** *(Before the invention of typewriters and printers, multiple copies of a book were written by hand. This took time and effort, and many mistakes were made. However, things changed during the Song Dynasty when a man called Bi Sheng invented moveable type printing.)*

5. **C. Gunpowder** *(Gunpowder is one of ancient China's most famous inventions. Interestingly, its discovery was an accident. According to legends, alchemists had been looking for a potion that would make people immortal. They mixed saltpeter, charcoal, and sulfur, hoping to find the secret to immortality, but they ended up discovering gunpowder.)*

Fill the Blanks

1. **Seismograph** *(Inventor Zhang Heng invented the seismograph during the Han Dynasty to determine earthquakes' directions. No one believed that this instrument could work. However, in 138 A.D., the seismograph was used to detect an earthquake in Longxi. . Once the news spread around the country, everyone became impressed with Zhang's invention.)*

2. **Acupuncture** *(Acupuncture is a technique that involves inserting needles into a person's body to relieve pain and help manage different diseases. It was very popular in ancient China to treat, diagnose, and prevent diseases.)*

3. **Alcohol** *(Alcohol, especially beer, was popular in ancient China and was even mentioned on oracle bones from the Song Dynasty. It was used as an offering for the ancestors.)*

4. **Seed drill** *(Seed drill was used to plant seeds into the soil. Before its invention, farmers planted seeds with their hands, which resulted in plants growing unevenly. The device had a huge impact on agriculture and made farmers' jobs much easier.)*

5. **Comets** *(Ancient China was one of the first cultures to study astronomy and observe the night sky. They crafted one of the oldest star maps in history. Ancient Chinese called comets "Broom stars" during the Han Dynasty. They believed that they were celestial brooms the gods used to sweep evil from heaven.)*

Short Answers

1. **Writing messages** (*Philosophers Lu Ban and Mozi invented the kite, which became a significant military instrument. It was similar to drones and was used to send gunpowder and messages and measure distance.*)

2. **Finding directions** (*The ancient Chinese used the compass in divination, fortune telling, and worshiping their gods. Sailors began using it in navigation and to find direction in the 11th or 12th century.*)

3. **Printing books** (*Woodblock printing helped spread information, news, and religious texts. It also made printing easier and cheaper as they could publish multiple copies in a short time.*)

4. **Blood Circulation** (*Huangdi Neijing is a traditional Chinese medical book that was written over 2000 years ago. The book described blood circulation as a continuous flow that never stops like a circle with no beginning or end.*)

5. **Its role in solar eclipse** (*Shi Shen was an ancient Chinese astronomer who discovered the moon's role in the solar system and how its light comes from the sun's reflection.*)

Picture-Based Query

1. **Chess** (*Military strategist and politician Han Xin invented Xiangqi or Chinese chess. During one of the wars, the soldiers were tired and homesick. To help raise his men's morale, Han invented Xiangqi.*)

2. **Seismograph** (*The device looks like an urn and is surrounded by eight metal dragon heads pointing in a different direction with a copper ball in each one's mouth. Below the dragons are eight copper toads with their mouths open. This device is sensitive to vibrations. During an earthquake, the dragon from which the direction the earthquake came would open its mouth and drop its ball into the toad below it.*)

3. **Arrows with gunpowder** (*Before gunpowder was used to make weapons, ancient Chinese used it to make fireworks and flares.*)

4. **Zhuge Liang** (*He was a general during the Han Dynasty, and he invented the one-wheeled wheelbarrow centuries before the Europeans did. His invention was intended to help the army with transportation. Similar to their other inventions, the Chinese kept*

the invention of the wheelbarrow a secret because it gave them an advantage over their enemies in battle.)

5. **Lu Ban** *(According to ancient Chinese legend, Lu Ban invented the umbrella during the late Spring and Autumn Period. It was made of silk, and only nobles and kings used it.)*

Global Influence

1. It isn't an exaggeration to say that the invention of paper has changed the world. It facilitates record-keeping and helps improve education by making writing and publishing books much easier. Paper also improved communication as people used it to send letters to one another. It also helps spread ideas and literature – and contributes to technological and cultural advancement. It is also used to create military maps and paper money.

2. Although acupuncture was invented centuries ago, it is still popular and a big part of alternative medicine. It is used to reduce discomfort associated with various conditions such as respiratory issues, neck pain, lower back pain, headaches, Fibromyalgia, dental pain, and chemotherapy.

3. The seismology was a great discovery that saved thousands of people's lives. The device allowed the government to monitor earthquakes and their directions so they could send assistance.

4. Gunpowder had a huge impact on the world. However, like any invention, it has its advantages and disadvantages. It helped develop mines, bombs, cannons, and rockets, which gave the ancient Chinese a huge advantage during battle. Gunpowder also led to the invention of weapons of war. However, many believe that this invention caused the death of millions of people worldwide throughout the years. Others argue that it gave countries the chance to protect themselves from invasion.

5. Before the compass, sailors relied on the position of the stars and the sun to find direction. However, the invention of the ancient Chinese compass made navigation much easier and more accurate. It also paved the way for more advanced and precise devices that had a huge impact on exploring and navigation.

Technological Timeline

1. Paper (105 A.D.), printing (960-1279 AD), gunpowder (1000 A.D.), and compass (1100 A.D.)

2. Alcohol (2000 B.C. − 1600 B.C.), umbrella (1st century B.C.), wheelbarrow (100 A.D.), and mechanical clock (725 A.D.).

3. Silk (3000-4000 B.C.), tea (2737 B.C.), acupuncture (2500 B.C.), and porcelain (581 - 618 AD).

4. Bronze (1700 B.C.), kite (475 BCE and 221 BCE), seismograph (132 A.D), and rocket (228 A.D.)

5. Fireworks (200 B.C.), paper money (9th century), cannons (12th-13th century), and toothbrushes (1498 AD)

Innovation Analysis

1. Many small farmers depended on silk for income. With the advancement of weaving techniques, Chinese silk's popularity expanded, and it became one of the most desired products in the ancient world and the country's biggest export, which contributed to its economic growth. Silk became so important that it gave its name to the popular trading route "Silk Road," which brought ancient China out of isolation, facilitated cultural exchange, and brought the country closer to other ancient civilizations.

2. The invention of paper money made trading much easier as it allowed merchants to travel long distances without carrying heavy coins, which could make the trip harder. Persian and European merchants discovered paper money on the Silk Road and spread it to their countries. Marco Polo learned about paper money while working for Khubilai Khan' during the Yuan Dynasty. He took this knowledge to the West and explained how paper money was used.

3. Gunpowder changed how wars were fought worldwide during the Middle Ages. The Song Dynasty's rulers recognized its power and used it in their battles against the Mongols. The Mongols were the first people to face advanced weapons made with gunpowder, such as flying fire. Historians believe that the new technology had a huge impact on both sides as it gave the ancient Chinese confidence and broke the Mongols' morale, leading to China's victory.

4. Paper and printing provided a cheaper and faster way to write and publish books. These inventions allowed for the spread of literary works and made books cheap and available for everyone, which helped fight illiteracy and increased education opportunities. When the knowledge of paper-making spread worldwide, it

allowed for the exchange of culture and intellectual ideas. Paper was used to preserve scientific knowledge, literature, and historical texts.

5. Europe imported over 70 million porcelain pieces from Asia. The West was in awe of its beauty and depth and started to study it and make their own. Many European craftspeople borrowed themes from ancient Chinese porcelain.

Chapter 9: Spiritual Paths: Buddhism, Taoism, and Confucianism

Ancient China was famous for its philosophical schools, which had a huge impact on the country's culture and society. In this chapter, you will walk a spiritual path with creative and interactive questions about Buddhism, Taoism, and Confucianism.

True or False

1. Confucius valued education and knowledge.

- True
- False

2. Confucius was against ancestor worship.

- True
- False

3. Confucius wrote all his teachings in one book.

- True
- False

4. Taoism focuses on a person's character, and Confucianism focuses on society.

- True
- False

5. Taoism believes that people are bad.

- True
- False

Multiple Choice

1. Which philosophy matches these statements: "'Go with the flow" and "Doing Nothing."

   A. Legalism

   B. Confucianism

   C. Buddhism

   D. Taoism

2. Which philosophy matches this statement: "Human beings are essentially bad and inherently selfish."

   A. Legalism

   B. Confucianism

   C. Buddhism

   D. Taoism

3. What did Confucius believe the role of a good ruler should be?

   A. To control his people

   B. To educate his people

   C. To expand his kingdom

   D. To punish his people

4. Which philosophy school describes the government as a family?

   A. Legalism

   B. Confucianism

   C. Buddhism

   D. Taoism

5. Which philosophy agrees with this statement: "What goes around, comes around"?

    A. Legalism

    B. Confucianism

    C. Buddhism

    D. Taoism

Fill in the Blanks

1. _____ philosophy teaches people to respect their elders.

2. _____ philosophy values simplicity.

3. Taoists don't believe in _____.

4. Buddhism began in _____.

5. Buddha called his teachings _____.

Short Answers

1. Who was China's greatest philosopher?

_____

_____

_____

2. Which school of philosophy was a favorite among many Chinese emperors?

_____

_____

_____

3. What is a good ruler according to Taoism?

_____

_____

_____

4. What is the oldest foreign religion in ancient China?

_____

_____

_____

5. What is one of Buddhism's main beliefs?

_____

_____

_____

Picture-Based Query

1. Identify this picture and what philosophy it is associated with.

Illustration 73

Response: _____.

2. What is this person doing, and which philosophy is it associated with?

Illustration 74

Response: _____.

3. What spiritual school does this temple belong to?

Illustration 75

Response: _____.

4. Who does this statue belong to?

Illustration 76

Response: _____.

5. What is the name of this book?

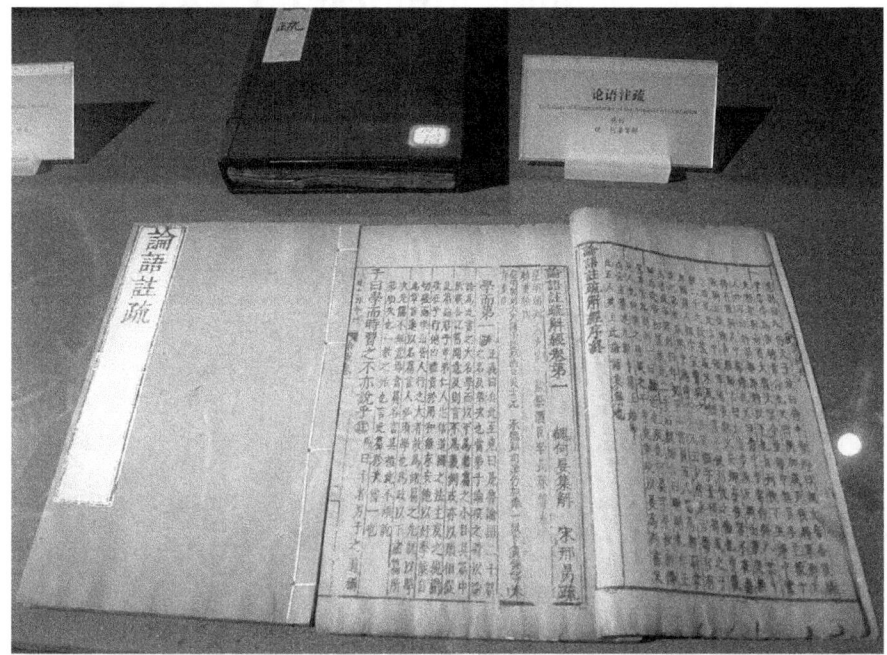

Illustration 77

Response: _____.

Modern Application

1. How would Confucian principles guide you in resolving a conflict with a friend?

_____

_____

_____

2. How would Taoist principles help you forgive someone who hurt your feelings?

_____

_____

_____

3. How would Buddhist principles help you feel better after getting bad news?

_____

_____

_____

4. How would you apply Confucian principles to your family?

_____

_____

_____

5. How would you apply Buddhist principles to help others?

_____

_____

_____

Philosophical Debate

1. Compare and contrast the views of Taoism and Buddhism on the concept of "balance in nature."

_____

_____

_____

2. Compare and contrast the views of Taoism and Confucianism on the concept of "being a good or a bad person."

_____

_____

_____

3. Compare and contrast the views of Taoism and Buddhism on the concept of "living a simple life."

_____

_____

_____

4. Compare and contrast the views of Confucianism and Buddhism on the concept of "greed."

_____

_____

_____

5. Compare and contrast the views of Buddhism and Taoism on the concept of "living a happy life."

_____

_____

_____

Belief System Analysis

1. Which aspects of Taoist philosophy can be seen in traditional Chinese medicine and practices?

_____

_____

_____

2. Which aspects of Confucianism philosophy can be seen in the study of ethics?

_____

_____

_____

3. How can Buddhism be used in self-reflection?

_____

_____

_____

4. Which aspects of Confucianism philosophy can improve society?

_____

_____

_____

5. Which aspects of Buddhism philosophy can be seen in modern psychology?

_____

_____

_____

Ethical Dilemma

1. Using Buddhist teachings, how would you address a modern social issue such as environmental conservation?

_____

_____

_____

2. Using Taoist teachings, how would you address a modern issue such as mental health?

_____

_____

_____

3. Using Confucius's teachings, how do you think rulers should govern countries?

_____

_____

_____

4. Using Buddhist teachings, how would you address a topic such as world peace?

_____

_____

_____

5. Using Buddhist teachings, how would you address a topic such as obsession with materialism?

_____

_____

_____

Cultural Impact

1. Discuss the influence of Confucianism on the ancient Chinese government and education systems.

_____

_____

_____

2. Discuss how Confucianism contradicted Legalism beliefs in ancient China.

_____

_____

_____

3. Discuss the impact of Buddhism on trade in ancient China.

_____

_____

_____

4. Discuss the impact of Taosim on ancient Chinese science.

_____

_____

_____

5. Discuss the influence of Confucianism on ancient Chinese art.

_____

_____

_____

Answer Key

True or False

1. True *(Confucius talked about the significance of education on many occasions. He believed that it could bring societal harmony and self-improvement. However, education is more than just learning and acquiring knowledge; it is also about improving one's morals and ethics. Confucius highly respected teachers because of their importance in educating young minds.)*

2. False *(Confucius believed that ancestor worship could bring harmony into one's life. He based this belief on filial piety, which teaches young people to respect their ancestors, parents, and elders.)*

3. False *(Confucius's teachings are found in nine books titled "Four Books and Five Classics," which are the foundation of Confucianism. They were the basis of the civil exams that took place in ancient China. Many historians believe that Confucius's students wrote all Of the books on Confucianism, but he never wrote down any of his teachings. Confucius didn't think his ideas were original or new, and he only passed on ancient Chinese philosophy.)*

4. True *(Taoism's teachings focus on the individual and encourage each person to live a simple life in harmony with nature. Confucianism guides societies to restore order by adopting certain virtues like respect, trust, and loyalty. However, Taoists believe that nature's rules are more important than people's rules. They disagreed with Confucius's teachings that stressed the significance of a civilized society and believed it to be unnatural.)*

5. False *(Taoists believed that people weren't bad, but their actions and behavior could be harmful. However, with the proper guidance and teachings, they could learn to be and do better.)*

Multiple Choice

1. D. Taoism *(Going with the flow is one of Taoism's main principles. It encourages people to be in harmony with any situation or event instead of resisting or overthinking. When things don't go as planned, one should go with the flow and change their course instead of getting sad or angry.)*

2. **A. Legalism** *(According to Legalism, people are bad and selfish. They aren't capable of doing good deeds or making any sacrifices unless they are forced to do so. A person might even kill another if it benefits them.)*

3. **B. To educate his people** *(Confucius believed that good rulers should educate their people by teaching them meditation. People should meditate when they face a problem instead of following rules that dictate what's right and what isn't. He also believed that emperors should lead by example. An ideal ruler should have certain virtues such as honesty and wisdom, and people should follow in his footsteps.)*

4. **B. Confucianism** *(Confucius believed that the relationship between family members should be a symbol of how the state and society should function. For instance, the emperor was similar to the father who loved and protected his family. The people were his children who respected and looked up to him.)*

5. **C. Buddhism** *(Buddhists believe in karma or what goes around comes around. Everything you do, good or bad, will have consequences. If you give to charity, good things will happen to you. If you steal, bad things will happen to you. In other words, good deeds are rewarded, and bad ones are punished.)*

Fill in the Blanks

1. **Confucianism** *(Confucius believed that a person could only be knowledgeable and successful when they ask the elderly for advice and follow their teachings.)*

2. **Taoism** *(Simplicity is about being real, natural, and true to yourself. It reflects Taoism's beliefs, which are effortless, spontaneous, and balanced. Living a simple life helps you avoid distractions and complications that can affect your relationship and harmony with nature.)*

3. **Strict laws** *(Taoist beliefs are against strict laws. Taoists believe that nature is in control of everything, which makes rules and laws unnecessary)*

4. **India** *(Buddhism originated in India in the late sixth century and then spread to China and the rest of the world.)*

5. **Dharma** *(Buddhism's teachings and beliefs explain the nature of the universe. The word "Dharma" translates to "to hold or support"*

because it upholds Buddhists, Buddhism, and the natural order of the universe. Buddhists should follow Dhamma's teachings.)

Short Answers

1. **Confucius** *(Confucius is China's greatest philosopher and first teacher. He spoke about the importance of education and wanted to make it available to everyone. He also played a big role in getting qualified individuals to work as teachers. Confucius also set moral, social, and ethical standards that became the foundation of Confucianism.)*

2. **Confucianism** *(Many Chinese emperors preferred Confucianism because of its principles that call for respecting the elderly and creating harmonious relationships between individuals.)*

3. **Supportive** *(Taoism's ideal rulers should follow the "Go with the flow" principle and let any situation run its course. They should only interfere when it's necessary. They should keep the country safe, peaceful, and prosperous, but they should never talk about or show off their accomplishments.)*

4. **Buddhism** *(In the early days, only foreign merchants and monks practiced Buddhism until it spread to China and became its main religion.)*

5. **Samsara** *(Buddhists believe that life is a cycle of birth, death, and rebirth. After a person dies, they are reborn as gods, demigods, humans, animals, ghosts, or hell creatures. Their rebirth depends on their karma. If their actions, thoughts, and intentions were good, they would have a good rebirth and vice versa.)*

Picture-Based Query

1. **Yin Yang/Taoism** *(It is an ancient philosophy that explains how the universe is ruled by opposite forces such as dark and night, female and male, and good and evil.)*

2. **Meditation/Buddhism** *(Meditation is a big part of Buddhism as it can bring a sense of calmness, balance, and peace, which can help a person reach enlightenment. Enlightenment is an experience that awakens your mind and frees you of hatred, greed, and suffering.)*

3. **Temple of Confucius** *(Legend says that when Confucius' mother was pregnant with him, a mythical creature called qilin visited her, Revealing that her unborn son would have a great future.)*

4. Buddha *(The word "Buddha" means "The enlightened one.")*

5. The Analects of Confucius *(It is a book about Confucius's life and teachings.)*

Philosophical Debate

1. Taoism explains that nature is balanced, and people should understand and respect it. Taoists live according to the Tao or the Way with the flow of nature. They believe that human life is a small part of the natural world, so it can only make sense when one lives in harmony with it and respects its cycle. Buddhism encourages its followers to live a simple and peaceful life. They should have a close relationship with nature that is based on mutual interaction and respect. A person's inner life and well-being are linked with the environment. If you take care of it, it will take care of you.

2. Confucius believed that all people are born good. However, they might stray away from their morals and ethics and make mistakes. Taoists believe that humans are neither good nor evil, but they can behave well or badly. Confucius stressed the significance of having morals and a good character. Being a decent person doesn't only affect you but the whole world as well. Taoism also encourages its followers to behave kindly toward others and stay away from bad behaviors such as lying and stealing.

3. Simplicity is one of Taoism's main principles. It encourages its followers to live a life that reflects the simplicity of nature. Buddhism teaches its followers that suffering lies in material desire and getting attached to temporary things. When one embraces simplicity, one will be able to live in the moment.

4. Confucianism warns people against greed, showing off, and materialism. Greedy and selfish people can bring imbalance to the universe, and they won't be able to live in harmony with themselves or nature. Buddhists believe that greedy people feel that they don't have enough and always want more. However, they can get rid of this feeling by practicing generosity and sharing what they have with others.

5. Confucius believed that real happiness lies in ethical pleasure. A person doesn't need to fulfill their every desire to be happy. They just need to have ethical needs and perfect virtues, which include great morals and being a good person. Buddhists believe that

peace of mind and staying away from materialistic desires can bring happiness to someone's life.

Belief System Analysis

1. Tai chi and qi gong (Chinese movement exercises), dietary therapy, tui na massage, Chinese herbal medicine, cupping, acupressure massage, and acupuncture.

2. Confucius believed that one can have ethics by living an honest life and having a good relationship with the people in one's life. When people have good morals and treat others kindly, they will have happy and healthy relationships, which will create a harmonious society.

3. Self-reflection is an effective technique that can help a person understand themselves better and live a balanced life. Meditation is one of the main aspects of Buddhism and helps clear a person's mind so they can look within and learn the truth about themselves.

4. Confucius believed that order could be restored to societies when individuals adopt certain virtues such as respecting the elderly, trustworthiness, and loyalty.

5. Many Buddhist ideas are relevant in modern psychology, such as mindfulness, peacefulness, compassion, kindness, and love, which can improve a person's mental health and well-being.

Culture Impact

1. Ancient empires such as the Han Dynasty adopted Confucianism because it allowed the government to maintain social order and helped spread morals such as ancestors' worship and respect for the elderly, which greatly influenced ancient Chinese society. The philosopher's impact was obvious in civil service exams, which required knowledge of Confucius's teachings. Confucius also influenced education by saying that every person had the right to learn, no matter what their class was.

2. According to Legalism, people are evil, selfish, and capable of committing terrible crimes. They need strict laws that punish them for bad behavior and reward them for doing the right thing. Confucianism contradicts these ideas by explaining that people are inherently good but can behave badly on occasion. However, they can improve and learn better behavior through education and adopting virtues such as respect and trust.

3. Buddhists built temples and monasteries along the Silk Road. They often bought incense oils, clothes, and other goods from merchants, which helped improve trade and the economy.

4. Taoists conducted various experiments to see the impact of medicine on humans and animals. They used this knowledge to find ways to prolong human lives. Their interest in immortality led them to learn about alchemy. Taoist alchemist Wei Boyang wrote one of the first books on alchemy during the Han Dynasty. Taoist Ge Hong wrote another book on the subject during the Jin Dynasty. Modern-day chemists and alchemists owe so much of their knowledge to ancient Chinese Taoists.

5. Confucius believed that art, music, and poetry were necessary for intellectual and moral development. Many ancient Chinese painters used art to teach moral lessons.

Chapter 10: The Silk Road: Crossroads of Culture and Trade

Trade was a big part of ancient China. It not only improved the country's economy but also introduced Chinese products to the world and strengthened its relationship with other countries. The Silk Road played a major role in trading and connecting China with Europe. It also became a cultural crossroad between the two regions. This chapter covers fun and exciting questions about trading and the Silk Road.

True or False

1. Merchants travel the entire distance of the Silk Road.

   - True
   - False

2. The Romans had never heard of silk until they discovered the Silk Road.

   - True
   - False

3. The Silk Road connected China to India.

   - True
   - False

4. The Chinese were the only ones who knew how to make silk.

- True
- False

5. The Silk Road connected four of the most powerful empires from the first to third centuries.

- True
- False

Multiple Choice

1. How did merchants travel on the Silk Road?

    A. On horses

    B. In a caravan of camels

    C. On foot

    D. On donkeys

2. What Chinese invention protected the Silk Road?

    A. Paper

    B. Bronze

    C. The Great Wall of China

    D. Gunpowder

3. Which famous explorer was known for taking the Silk Road?

    A. Marco Polo

    B. Christopher Colombus

    C. Jacques Cousteau

    D. All of the above

4. What were the most traded items between the East and West?

    A. Horses and cows

    B. Milk and cheese

    C. Iron and bronze

    D. Gunpowder and paper

5. What invention enabled a wider exchange of information between cultures?

    A. Carriages

    B. Movable type printing

    C. Writing

    D. Planes

Fill the Blanks

1. The Romans called China _____, meaning "Land of Silk."

2. The _____ led to open trade between China and other countries.

3. _____ came up with the name "The Silk Road."

4. The Silk Road helped create _____ for many people in different countries.

5. The Silk Road is defined as _____.

Short Answers

1. Besides goods, what else did the Chinese trade with Europe?

_____

_____

_____

2. Why was it difficult for merchants to travel the entire Silk Road?

_____

_____

_____

3. How did the closure of the Silk Road affect exploration?

_____

_____

_____

4. How did the Silk Road promote cultural exchange?

_____

_____

_____

5. How did the knowledge of silk spread to other countries?

_____

_____

_____

Picture-Based Query

1. Name this famous route and the river by its side.

Illustration 78

Response: _____.

2. Name this famous explorer.

Illustration 79

Response: _____.

3. What breed of horse is this, and what dynasty does it belong to?

Illustration 80

Response: _____.

4. Name two of these famous goods that were often traded along the Silk Road.

Illustration 81

Response: _____.

5. Trace the route of the Silk Road and identify key cities that were pivotal to its operation.

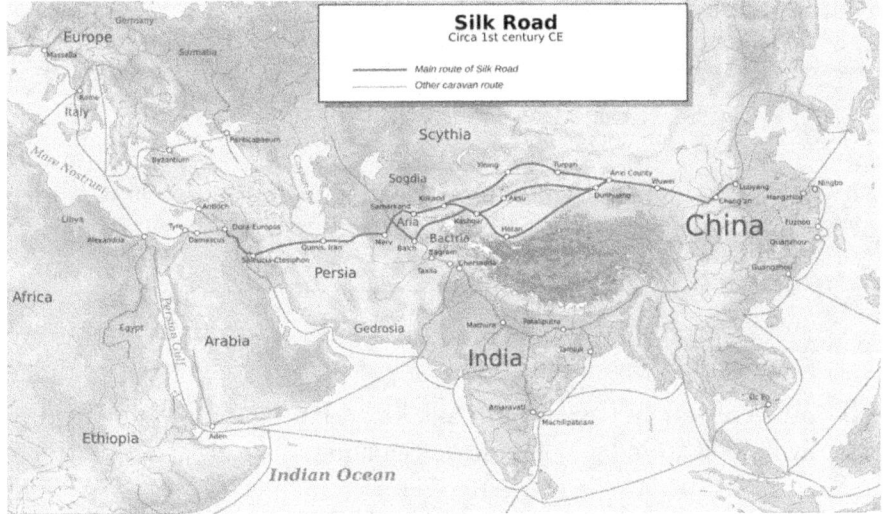

Illustration 82

Response: _____.

Trader's Dilemma

1. If you were a merchant on the Silk Road, what goods would you trade, and what challenges would you face on your journey?

_____

_____

_____

2. If you were a merchant on the Silk Road and faced thieves with weapons trying to steal your goods, how would you handle the situation?

_____

_____

_____

3. If you were a European merchant, how would you prepare for a trip to China? What would you learn about the culture?

_____

_____

_____

4. If you were a Chinese merchant, what goods would you take to Europe to introduce them to your culture?

_____

_____

_____

5. If you were a merchant on the Silk Road and got lost. What would you do?

_____

_____

_____

6. If you were a merchant on the Silk Road and some of your men got seriously ill, how would you handle the situation?

_____

_____

_____

7. If you were a Chinese merchant in ancient China and met European merchants who wanted to know the secret behind making paper or silk, what would you do to protect the secret?

_____

_____

_____

8. If you were an ancient Chinese merchant and wanted to start a culture exchange with England, which philosophy book would you take to spread its teachings and why?

_____

_____

_____

9. If you were an ancient Chinese merchant visiting a country for the first time, what gift would you take to its ruler to establish a relationship with them?

_____

_____

_____

10. Imagine you took longer on the road, and some of your goods started to go bad. You aren't sure whether the rest of your goods will survive the journey or not. What would you do?

_____

_____

_____

Cultural Exchange Puzzle

Match each item to the Dynasty that introduced it on the Silk Road.

1. The Han Dynasty	
	Illustration 83
2. Qin and Han Dynasties	
	Illustration 84
3. Tang Dynasty	
	Illustration 85

4. The Shang Dynasty	 **Illustration 86**
5. The Yuan Dynasty	 **Illustration 87**

Historical Impact Analysis

1. Discuss how the Silk Road facilitated the spread of Buddhism from India to China.

_____

_____

_____

2. Discuss how the Silk Road facilitated the spread of Taoism across Asia.

_____

_____

_____

3. Discuss how the Silk Road facilitated the spread of technology worldwide.

_____

_____

_____

4. Discuss how the Silk Road facilitated the spread of literature worldwide.

_____

_____

_____

5. Discuss how the Silk Road brought China out of isolation.

_____

_____

_____

Interactive Exploration

1. Choose an item commonly traded on the Silk Road and describe its journey from origin to destination, including the cultures it passed through.

_____

_____

_____

2. Imagine you are a Buddhist monk. Describe your journey from India to China and your interactions with people from different cultures.

_____

_____

_____

3. Imagine you are an ancient Chinese merchant who has just arrived in Europe. Describe your experience and interactions.

_____

_____

_____

4. Imagine you are trading on the Silk Road. You and your men took a break from your journey near the river. You met other merchants from India. Discuss your interactions and culture exchange.

_____

_____

_____

5. Imagine you are a European ruler, and merchants from China come to you with gifts and goods. Discuss your interactions and mention the goods they brought you.

_____

_____

_____

Answer Key

1. False *(Merchants only traveled part of the Silk Route and sold their goods to other traders on the road. Traveling the entire route was challenging due to the poor conditions of the roads. It was also very long with mountains, plains, valleys, and rivers, making the journey exhausting and dangerous.)*

2. False *(The Romans knew about silk through trading with China and other civilizations before they discovered the Silk Road. The famous route made trade easier between the East and West but didn't introduce the fabric to the Romans.)*

3. True *(The connection between the two countries led to the spread of Buddhism from India to China.)*

4. True *(Similar to paper, the Chinese kept their knowledge of making silk a secret. Silk was one of the most valuable fabrics at the time. It was a favorite among kings and queens worldwide. The Chinese were aware of its popularity and kept the process of making it to themselves. If anyone tried to reveal it, they were severely punished.)*

5. True *(The Kushans in Central Asia, the Parthian monarchy in the Far and Middle East, the Roman Empire, and the Han Dynasty in China traded freely and peacefully along the Silk Road.)*

Multiple Choice

1. B. In a caravan with camels *(Merchants traveled together in caravans for protection as there were robbers on the Silk Road. Traveling in groups helped them defeat thieves and kept them safe until they reached their destination.)*

2. C. The Great Wall of China *(The wall protected people from nomads and harassment, prevented invaders from entering the country, and protected trade routes from thieves. Ancient China would have succeeded in protecting itself and the Silk Route by allying with neighboring countries to create a powerful defense system that kept China safe. However, this wasn't always possible, which made the Great Wall its only defense system. Although the Great Wall of China is an architectural masterpiece and a world wonder, it was flawed. Some of China's enemies found weaknesses *that enabled them to invade the country.)*

3. **A. Marco Polo** *(He was the most famous European explorer to use the Silk Road, which took him to China.)*

4. **D. Gunpowder and paper** *(Inventing paper showed the world that China was technologically advanced. Interestingly, archaeologists found that inventing early forms of paper was accidental. After the ancient Chinese washed clothes made of hemp, they would leave them to dry. Clothes that were left for too long to dry formed a residue that turned into a new material (paper) after pressing. Paper and gunpowder are two of China's four great inventions, including printing and the compass.)*

5. **B. Movable type printing** *(This invention made books more accessible and cheaper, which made it easier to spread Chinese culture worldwide.)*

Fill in the Blanks

1. **Serica** *(The Romans also called China "Sinae," meaning "The land of Qin," referring to China's first imperial dynasty.)*

2. **Blood-sweating horses** *(They are also called "Ferghana horses." They are small, inanimate horses made of clay that originated from Central Asia and were one of ancient China's main imports. According to ancient Chinese legend, these horses were extremely powerful and sweat blood, leading many to believe they were divine.)*

3. **Ferdinand von Richthofen** *(In 1877, the German traveler and geographer gave the network of roads between Asia and Europe the name "Silk Road" because the production of silk originated in China and was one of its most valuable and popular goods.)*

4. **Jobs** *(The Silk Road helped provide many job opportunities in different countries. Since trading was expanding, businesses employed more people to make goods, and merchants hired craftspeople to build enough caravans to transport the goods.)*

5. **Network of roads** *(Unlike what the name suggests, the Silk Road is neither a single route nor a road. It is best described as a network of routes. This is why some historians don't prefer the name "Silk Road" and use "Silk Routes" since it's more accurate.)*

Short Answers

1. **Ideas** *(The Silk Road can be described as a cultural hub since people from all over the world met and interacted on its routes, which provided the opportunity for an exchange of ideas and culture.)*

2. **Bad weather conditions** *(Extreme heat or freezing cold made it impossible for merchants to travel the entire Silk Road.)*

3. **It began the Age of Discovery** *(The closure of the Silk Road began the Age of Exploration, AKA the Age of Discovery. European merchants and travelers turned to water instead of land to reach Asia. This provided an opportunity for cultural exchange between Europe and other countries. Each could share its religion, traditions, customs, technology, and ideas with the other.)*

4. **Music, art, and theater** *(Merchants, travelers, and explorers on the Silk Road were introduced to different types of music, art, theater, and literature by observing and interacting with people on the road and learning about different cultures, backgrounds, and ideas.)*

5. **By sending them as gifts to other rulers** *(Chinese emperors sent silk as gifts to rulers from different countries, which helped spread knowledge of silk worldwide.)*

Picture-Based Query

1. **Silk Route by the side of the Indus River** *(The road is over 2000 years old, and there were five Silk Routes from China alone.)*

2. **Ferdinand von Richthofen** *(Ferdinand's biggest contribution was his research on yellow soil in China).*

3. **Ferghana horse from the Tang Dynasty** *(This type of horse is extinct.)*

4. **Spices and tea** *(They are still China's two biggest exports).*

5. **Luoyang, Chang'an, Wuwei, Anxi County, Dunhuang, Turpan, Yining, Aksu, Hotan, Kashgar, Kokand, Samarkand, Merv, Qumis Iran, Seleucia-Ctesiphon, and Dura-Europos.**

Cultural Exchange Puzzle

1. The Han Dynasty/Silk.

2. Qin and Han Dynasties/ Spices.

3. Tang Dynasty/Jade.

4. The Shang Dynasty/Bronze.

5. The Yuan Dynasty/Blue and white porcelain.

Historical Impact Analysis

1. Trading along the Silk Road helped spread Buddhist teachings from India to China and made it one of the biggest religions in the world. Five Buddhist schools were located along the Silk Road, which allowed merchants to trade and interact with Buddhist monks. Buddhism teaches its followers to be kind and generous. They welcomed any contribution from merchants on the Silk Road. The monks thanked them for their kind gifts by providing spiritual guidance.

2. Buddhism and Taoism interacted with each other in China during the third century. Taoism spread in China and Asia the same way Buddhism did by building religious facilities for merchants and travelers to learn about the religion on the Silk Road. Taoism had a huge impact on many religious beliefs, including Buddhism. Many Buddhist temples include Taoism chapels. The Buddhist tradition "Chinese Chan," which many know as "Zen," owes its teachings to Buddhist Taoism Syncretism.

3. Many ancient cultures influenced one another's scientific and technological discoveries. The Silk Road played a major role in bringing China closer to other ancient cultures. Merchants didn't only trade goods with one another – but also the knowledge and technology that went into making them. There was also an exchange of agricultural practices and knowledge of new animal breeds, plants, and crops. They also learned from each other crafts techniques for ceramics, textiles, and glass and the technology that went into their production.

4. The Silk Road also helped spread stories and other literary works that diplomats, monks, travelers, pilgrims, and scholars shared on the road. Scholars who worked or lived on the Silk Road translated many of these literary works to bring different cultures together.

5. Ancient China was isolated due to its geography, which was surrounded by seas, mountains, and deserts. Although they protected the country from foreign invasions, they isolated it from the rest of the world. The Silk Road connected China with other civilizations through fascinating cultures, religions, ideas, and technological exchanges with other countries.

Conclusion

Congratulations, you have finished the book and answered 500 trivia questions about ancient China. Do you feel that you have gained more knowledge after reading? Are you an ancient China expert now?

The book took you on a journey through nine of ancient China's most influential dynasties. You discovered how emperors rose to power and how dynasties fell. You learned about ancient China's many inventions and how they influenced many discoveries in Europe and the world.

Through the power of imagination, you traveled back in time and learned about ancient China's different philosophies and religions. You walked into the footsteps of merchants and traded on the Silk Road - and spent a day as an ancient Chinese child.

You answered different types of questions that allowed you to think, use your imagination, and put yourself in various scenarios. You became a philosopher who was stuck in an ethical dilemma and an inventor who was looking for ways to use his invention.

History is filled with lessons, and you saw the rise and fall of ancient Chinese rulers and learned from their mistakes. You were introduced to different schools of philosophy that will help expand your mind and thoughts.

Although the book is over, learning never ends. Keep reading and acquiring new information about your favorite topics.

If you enjoyed this book, a review on Amazon would be greatly appreciated because it would mean a lot to hear from you.

To leave a review:
1. Open your camera app.
2. Point your mobile device at the QR code.
3. The review page will appear in your web browser.

Thanks for your support!

Check out another book in the series

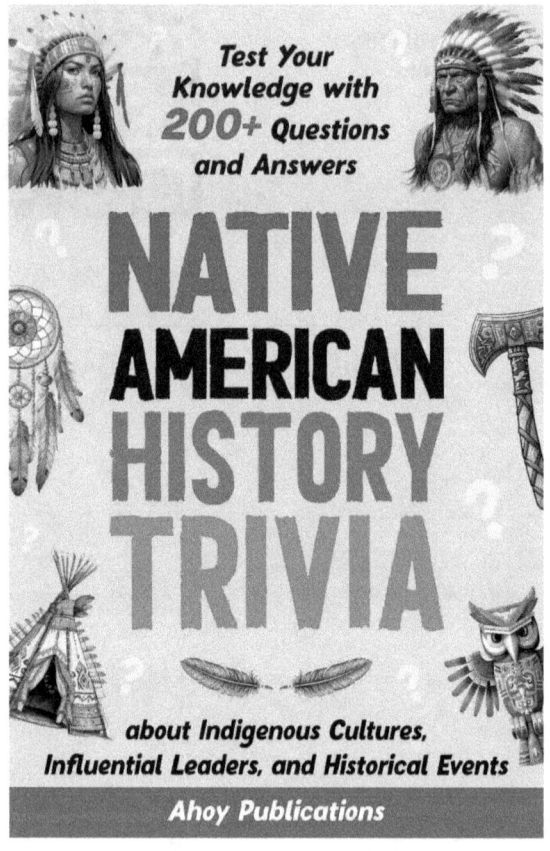

Welcome Aboard, Check Out This Limited-Time Free Bonus!

Ahoy, reader! Welcome to the Ahoy Publications family, and thanks for snagging a copy of this book! Since you've chosen to join us on this journey, we'd like to offer you something special.

Check out the link below for a FREE e-book filled with delightful facts about American History.

But that's not all - you'll also have access to our exclusive email list with even more free e-books and insider knowledge. Well, what are ye waiting for? Click the link below to join and set sail toward exciting adventures in American History.

Access your bonus here
https://ahoypublications.com/
Or, Scan the QR code!

References

10 Facts About the Yuan Dynasty, Highlights of Yuan Dynasty. (n.d.). Www.chinahighlights.com. https://www.chinahighlights.com/travelguide/china-history/yuan-dynasty-facts.htm#google_vignette

4,000-year-old palace discovered in central China. (2023, December 31). The Jerusalem Post | JPost.com. https://www.jpost.com/archaeology/article-780185

A history of Chinese tattoos and Chinese tattooing traditions[1]-Chinadaily.com.cn. (n.d.). Www.chinadaily.com.cn. https://www.chinadaily.com.cn/life/2011-03/15/content_12175139.htm

A quote by Gautama Buddha. (n.d.). Www.goodreads.com. https://www.goodreads.com/quotes/3181192-in-the-end-only-three-things-matter-how-much-you

Acupuncture - Mayo Clinic. (2024, April 20). Www.mayoclinic.org. https://www.mayoclinic.org/tests-procedures/acupuncture/about/pac-20392763

Admiral Zheng He's Voyages to the "West Oceans." (n.d.). Association for Asian Studies. https://www.asianstudies.org/publications/eaa/archives/admiral-zheng-hes-voyages-to-the-west-oceans

Advancements Under the Shang | Early World Civilizations. (n.d.). Courses.lumenlearning.com. https://courses.lumenlearning.com/atd-herkimer-worldcivilization/chapter/advancements-under-the-shang

Amaro, A. M. (2023). RITUALS OF LIFE AND DEATH IN ANCIENT CHINA. Icm.gov.mo. https://www.icm.gov.mo/rc/viewer/20018/992

American Numismatic Association. (n.d.). Chinese Paper Currency. American Numismatic Association. https://www.money.org/money-museum/virtual-exhibits-hom-case16

An introduction to the Ming dynasty (1368–1644) (article). (n.d.). Khan Academy. https://www.khanacademy.org/humanities/art-asia/imperial-china/ming-dynasty/a/an-introduction-to-the-ming-dynasty-13681644

Analyzing the Social Structure of Ancient China. (n.d.). Study.com. https://study.com/skill/practice/analyzing-the-social-structure-of-ancient-china-questions.html

Ancient China Geography | Facts, Isolation & Location. (n.d.). Study.com. https://study.com/academy/lesson/how-geography-isolated-ancient-china.html

Ancient China Test Review | Quizizz. (n.d.). Quizizz.com. https://quizizz.com/admin/quiz/5a689b9180bf2a001c3451fd/ancient-china-test-review

Ancient China: Xia Dynasty. (2019). Ducksters.com. https://www.ducksters.com/history/china/xia_dynasty.php

Ancient China: Yuan Dynasty. (2019). Ducksters.com. https://www.ducksters.com/history/china/yuan_dynasty.php

Ancient Chinese Kites for Kids - Ancient China for Kids. (n.d.). China.mrdonn.org. https://china.mrdonn.org/kites.html

Ancient Chinese Philosophies | 77 plays | Quizizz. (n.d.). Quizizz.com. https://quizizz.com/admin/quiz/586daaacbb5ddb7920e5dbcf/ancient-chinese-philosophies

Ancient Chinese Seismometers Used Dragons and Toads. (n.d.). Kids Discover Online. https://online.kidsdiscover.com/quickread/ancient-chinese-seismometer-used-dragons-and-toads

Andrews, E. (2014, April 29). 10 Things You May Not Know about Genghis Khan. History; A&E Television Networks. https://www.history.com/news/10-things-you-may-not-know-about-genghis-khan

Andrews, E. (2018, August 31). 11 Things You May Not Know About Marco Polo. HISTORY. https://www.history.com/news/11-things-you-may-not-know-about-marco-polo

Art under the Ming Dynasty | Early World Civilizations. (n.d.). Courses.lumenlearning.com. https://courses.lumenlearning.com/atd-herkimer-worldcivilization/chapter/art-under-the-ming-dynasty/

Asia. (2024). Asia for Educators | Columbia University. Columbia.edu. https://afe.easia.columbia.edu/special/china_1000bce_confucius_intro.htm

Attraction. (n.d.). R.visitbeijing.com.cn. https://r.visitbeijing.com.cn/attraction/10

Barksdale, N. (2018, October 9). 7 Things You May Not Know About the Ming Dynasty. HISTORY. https://www.history.com/news/7-things-you-may-not-know-about-the-ming-dynasty

Barnwell, Z. (n.d.). Zhou Dynasty | 170 plays | Quizizz. Quizizz.com. https://quizizz.com/admin/quiz/61808427657fc2001d51b145/zhou-dynasty?fromSearch=true&source=

BBC - Religions - Taoism: Taoist ethics. (n.d.). Www.bbc.co.uk. https://www.bbc.co.uk/religion/religions/taoism/taoethics/ethics_1.shtml

BBC. (2023). Rebirth - Buddhist beliefs - Edexcel - GCSE Religious Studies Revision - Edexcel. BBC Bitesize. https://www.bbc.co.uk/bitesize/guides/zf8g4qt/revision/8

Beijing's Ancient Observatory. (2010). NASA Blueshift. https://asd.gsfc.nasa.gov/blueshift/index.php/2010/08/20/maggies-blog-beijings-ancient-observatory/

Belief Systems Along the Silk Road. (n.d.). Asia Society. https://asiasociety.org/education/belief-systems-along-the-silk-road

Bevan, R. (2022a, January 26). 10 Facts About Confucius. History Hit. https://www.historyhit.com/facts-about-confucius/

Bevan, R. (2022b, February 2). 10 Facts About the Tang Dynasty. History Hit. https://www.historyhit.com/facts-about-the-tang-dynasty/

Beyer, G. (2024, April 11). 15 Facts About Genghis Khan & His Legacy. TheCollector. https://www.thecollector.com/genghis-khan-facts/

Bileta, V. (2022a, November 5). The 4 Powerful Empires of the Silk Road. TheCollector. https://www.thecollector.com/four-empires-silk-road/

Bileta, V. (2022b, November 27). The Seven Voyages of Zheng He: When China Ruled the Seas. TheCollector. https://www.thecollector.com/zheng-he-seven-voyages/

Bristol, U. of. (n.d.). Death and Dying in Buddhism. Www.bristol.ac.uk. https://www.bristol.ac.uk/religion/buddhist-centre/projects/bdr/chaplains/online-guide.html

Brown, L. (2016, November 6). Drinking Wine in Ancient China. JSTOR Daily. https://daily.jstor.org/wine-in-ancient-china/

Brown, T., & Lai, S. (2006, November). The Shang Dynasty, 1600 to 1050 BCE. Spice.fsi.stanford.edu. https://spice.fsi.stanford.edu/docs/the_shang_dynasty_1600_to_1050_bce

Buddha And The Path To Happiness - An Overview. (n.d.). Www.pursuit-of-Happiness.org. https://www.pursuit-of-happiness.org/history-of-happiness/buddha

Buddhism as a world religion: The Senior Phase Context. (n.d.). https://education.gov.scot/media/1dofdmp4/rme18-buddhism-senior-phase-context.pdf

Buddhist and non buddhist symbols in Mongolia : endless knot (ulzii), soyombo... - By Mongolia Travel and Tours. (n.d.). Www.mongolia-Travel-And-Tours.com. https://www.mongolia-travel-and-tours.com/symbols-mongolia.html#:~:text=The%20Soyombo%2C%20flag%20symbol%20of%20Mongolia&text=Fire%20is%20a%20general%20symbol

Byrne, S. (n.d.). Chinese Dynasties 1: Xia, Shang & Early Zhou | Quizizz. Quizizz.com. Retrieved July 4, 2024, from https://quizizz.com/admin/quiz/5d6749c17a52a1001d868666/chinese-dynasties-1-xia-shang-early-zhou

c. 1045 BC: Zhou kings introduce concept of Heaven (Tian), Mandate of Heaven, Son of Heaven | Chinese 110 | Timeline. (n.d.). Academics.wellesley.edu. Retrieved July 7, 2024, from http://academics.wellesley.edu/knapp/Chin110/Timeline/StudentResponses/Zhou/1045_kings_heaven.html

Campbell, D. R. (n.d.). The Fall of the Han Dynasty (article). Khan Academy. https://www.khanacademy.org/humanities/whp-origins/era-4-regional/41-systems-collapse-betaa/a/read-the-fall-of-the-han-dynasty-beta

Cartwright, M. (n.d.-a). Religion in the Mongol Empire. World History Encyclopedia. https://www.worldhistory.org/article/1469/religion-in-the-mongol-empire/#:~:text=Tibetan%20Buddhism%20was%20made%20the

Cartwright, M. (n.d.-b). The Mongol Invasions of Japan, 1274 & 1281 CE. World History Encyclopedia. Retrieved July 14, 2024, from https://www.worldhistory.org/article/1415/the-mongol-invasions-of-japan-1274--1281-ce/#:~:text=and%20caused%20havoc.-

Cartwright, M. (2017a, July 12). Chang'an. Www.worldhistory.org. https://www.worldhistory.org/Chang

Cartwright, M. (2017b, July 12). Warring States Period. World History Encyclopedia. https://www.worldhistory.org/Warring_States_Period/#:~:text=The%20Warring%20States%20period%20(481

Cartwright, M. (2017c, July 13). Chariots in Ancient Chinese Warfare. World History Encyclopedia. https://www.worldhistory.org/article/1091/chariots-in-ancient-chinese-warfare/#google_vignette

Cartwright, M. (2017d, July 17). Crossbows in Ancient Chinese Warfare. World History Encyclopedia. https://www.worldhistory.org/article/1098/crossbows-in-ancient-chinese-warfare/

Cartwright, M. (2017e, July 25). Mandate of Heaven. World History Encyclopedia. https://www.worldhistory.org/Mandate_of_Heaven/

Cartwright, M. (2017f, July 28). Silk in Antiquity. World History Encyclopedia. https://www.worldhistory.org/Silk/#:~:text=Silk%20is%20a%20fabric%20first

Cartwright, M. (2017g, September 14). Achievements of the Han Dynasty. World History Encyclopedia. https://www.worldhistory.org/article/1119/achievements-of-the-han-dynasty/

Cartwright, M. (2017h, September 15). Paper in Ancient China. World History Encyclopedia. https://www.worldhistory.org/article/1120/paper-in-ancient-china/#:~:text=The%20invention%20of%20paper%20greatly

Cartwright, M. (2017i, September 22). Sui Dynasty. World History Encyclopedia. https://www.worldhistory.org/Sui_Dynasty/

Cartwright, M. (2017j, September 27). Foot-Binding. World History Encyclopedia. https://www.worldhistory.org/Foot-Binding/

Cartwright, M. (2017k, October 11). The Art of the Tang Dynasty. World History Encyclopedia. https://www.worldhistory.org/article/1130/the-art-of-the-tang-dynasty/

Cartwright, M. (2017l, October 16). Ancient Chinese Calligraphy. World History Encyclopedia. https://www.worldhistory.org/Chinese_Calligraphy/#:~:text=Definition&text=Calligraphy%20established%20itself%20as%20the

Cartwright, M. (2017m, October 19). Women in Ancient China. World History Encyclopedia. https://www.worldhistory.org/article/1136/women-in-ancient-china/#google_vignette

Cartwright, M. (2018, May 16). Yin and Yang. World History Encyclopedia. https://www.worldhistory.org/Yin_and_Yang/

Cartwright, M. (2019a, February 6). Ming Dynasty. World History Encyclopedia. https://www.worldhistory.org/Ming_Dynasty/#google_vignette

Cartwright, M. (2019b, February 7). The Seven Voyages of Zheng He. World History Encyclopedia. https://www.worldhistory.org/article/1334/the-seven-voyages-of-zheng-he/

Cartwright, M. (2019c, February 8). The Civil Service Examinations of Imperial China. World History Encyclopedia. https://www.worldhistory.org/article/1335/the-civil-service-examinations-of-imperial-china/

Cartwright, M. (2019d, February 12). Marco Polo. World History Encyclopedia. https://www.worldhistory.org/Marco_Polo/

Cartwright, M. (2019e, February 13). Hongwu Emperor. World History Encyclopedia. https://www.worldhistory.org/Hongwu_Emperor/

Cartwright, M. (2019f, July 2). The Mongol Invasions of Japan, 1274 & 1281 CE. World History Encyclopedia. https://www.worldhistory.org/article/1415/the-mongol-invasions-of-japan-1274--1281-ce/

Cartwright, M. (2019g, September 18). Xanadu. World History Encyclopedia. https://www.worldhistory.org/Xanadu/

Centre, U. W. H. (n.d.). Yin Xu. UNESCO World Heritage Centre. https://whc.unesco.org/en/list/1114/#:~:text=The%20archaeological%20site%20o f%20Yin

CGTN. (2023, May 20). Why Chinese emperors from ethnic minorities respect Confucius. News.cgtn.com. https://news.cgtn.com/news/2023-05-20/Why-Chinese-emperors-from-ethnic-minorities-respect-Confucius-1jXqIItVKFg/index.html#:~:text=Ideologies%20shared%20by%20both%20ruling %20class%20and%20common%20people&text=Confucianism%20was%20widely %20embraced%20by

Chen, L., Cohen, S., Song, E., & Tsoy, S. (n.d.-a). Education and the Arts. THE TANG DYNASTY. https://legitsourceforyourtangdynastyessays.weebly.com/education-and-the-arts.html

Chen, L., Cohen, S., Song, E., & Tsoy, S. (n.d.-b). Social Structure. THE TANG DYNASTY. https://legitsourceforyourtangdynastyessays.weebly.com/social-structure.html#:~:text=Social%20structure%20in%20the%20Tang

Chi -hua, W. (1981). BASIC FOREIGN-POLICY ATTITUDES OF THE EARLY MING DYNASTY. Ming Studies, 1981(1), 65–80. https://doi.org/10.1179/014703781788764829

China Han Dynasty Quiz - Trivia & Questions. (n.d.). Www.proprofs.com. Retrieved July 9, 2024, from https://www.proprofs.com/quiz-school/story.php?title=china-han-dynasty-quiz

China Qin Dynasty Quiz - Trivia & Questions. (n.d.). Www.proprofs.com. Retrieved July 9, 2024, from https://www.proprofs.com/quiz-school/story.php?title=china-qin-dynasty-quiz

China Silk Road Quiz - Trivia & Questions. (n.d.). Www.proprofs.com. Retrieved July 20, 2024, from https://www.proprofs.com/quiz-school/story.php?title=china-silk-road-quiz

Chinese Funeral Traditions. (n.d.). Chapel of the Chimes Oakland. https://oakland.chapelofthechimes.com/resources/chinese-funeral-traditions#:~:text=After%20death%2C%20relatives%20and%20friends

Chinese Inventions. (n.d.). Asia Society. https://asiasociety.org/education/chinese-inventions#:~:text=Many%20are%20surprised%20to%20realize

Chinese jade: an introduction (article). (n.d.). Khan Academy. https://www.khanacademy.org/humanities/art-asia/imperial-china/neolithic-art-china/a/chinese-jade-an-introduction#:~:text=Jade%20was%20worn%20by%20kings

Chinese Merchants: Definition & Importance. (n.d.). Vaia. Retrieved July 9, 2024, from https://www.vaia.com/en-us/explanations/history/modern-world-history/chinese-merchants/#:~:text=Merchants%20were%20the%20next%20class

Chinese Paper making: History, Techniques. (n.d.). Vaia. Retrieved July 24, 2024, from https://www.vaia.com/en-us/explanations/chinese/chinese-vocabulary/chinese-paper-making/#:~:text=Chinese%20paper%20making%20revolutionised%20communication

Chinese Paper making: History, Techniques | StudySmarter. (n.d.). StudySmarter UK. Retrieved July 24, 2024, from https://www.studysmarter.co.uk/explanations/chinese/chinese-vocabulary/chinese-paper-making/#:~:text=Paper%20Making%20and%20the%20Spread%20of%20Culture&text=One%20of%20the%20most%20significant

Chinese Porcelain | Silk Roads Programme. (n.d.). En.unesco.org. https://en.unesco.org/silkroad/content/chinese-porcelain#:~:text=Porcelain%20is%20the%20creative%20fruit

Chinese Tea - china.org.cn. (n.d.). Www.china.org.cn. http://www.china.org.cn/learning_chinese/Chinese_tea/2011-07/15/content_22999489.htm#:~:text=In%20the%20Tang%20Dynasty%20(618

Clark ,J., & Bos, S. (1970, January 1). Top 10 Ancient Chinese Inventions. HowStuffWorks. https://science.howstuffworks.com/innovation/inventions/10-ancient-chinese-inventions.htm#pt1

Clemons, L. (n.d.). Zhou Dynasty | 680 plays | Quizizz. Quizizz.com. Retrieved July 5, 2024, from https://quizizz.com/admin/quiz/5a62035cef58a9001b07c964/zhou-dynasty?fromSearch=true&source=

Confucianism In Education: Philosophy & Values. (n.d.). Vaia. Retrieved July 21, 2024, from https://www.vaia.com/en-us/explanations/chinese/chinese-social-issues/confucianism-in-education/#:~:text=Confucius%2C%20a%20teacher%20and%20philosopher

Confucius' Ideas on Family & Society Video. (2013). Confucius' Ideas on Family & Society - Video & Lesson Transcript | Study.com. Study.com. https://study.com/academy/lesson/confucius-ideas-on-family-society.html#:~:text=Confucianism%20uses%20the%20family%20as

Cowrie-shell coin, earliest coins of China, Shang dynasty, c.1766-1154. (n.d.). NumisMall.com. Retrieved July 4, 2024, from https://www.numismall.com/products/cowrie-shell-coin-earliest-coins-of-china-shang-dynasty-c-1766-1154-bc-hartill-1-11#:~:text=In%20the%2014th%20century%20BC

Cromwell, S. (2020, May 21). China: Make Your Own Paper. Timothy S. Y. Lam Museum of Anthropology. https://lammuseum.wfu.edu/2020/05/china-make-your-own-paper/#:~:text=Traditionally%2C%20writing%20was%20done%20by

Cultural Selection: Illustrations of Literary Exchange along the Silk Roads | Silk Roads Programme. (n.d.). En.unesco.org. https://en.unesco.org/silkroad/content/cultural-selection-illustrations-literary-exchange-along-silk-roads#:~:text=The%20Silk%20Roads%20facilitated%20the

D'Angelo, D. (n.d.). Confucius Said | Ohio University. Www.ohio.edu. https://www.ohio.edu/cis/confucius-said#:~:text=In%20order%20to%20be%20successful

Daley, B. (2014, January 9). Marco Polo - the man who brought China to Europe. Www.europeana.eu. https://www.europeana.eu/en/stories/marco-polo-the-man-who-brought-china-to-europe

Decline of the Yuan Dynasty | World Civilization. (n.d.). Courses.lumenlearning.com. https://courses.lumenlearning.com/suny-hccc-worldcivilization/chapter/decline-of-the-yuan-dynasty/#:~:text=From%20the%20late%201340s%20onward

Department of Asian Art. (2019). Northern Song Dynasty (960–1127). Metmuseum.org. https://www.metmuseum.org/toah/hd/nsong/hd_nsong.htm

Department of Asian Art. (2020). Shang and Zhou Dynasties: The Bronze Age of China. Metmuseum.org. https://www.metmuseum.org/toah/hd/shzh/hd_shzh.htm#:~:text=The%20era%20of%20the%20Shang

Des Marais, S. (2018, June 9). How To Go With The Flow In Life: 12 Tips. Psych Central. https://psychcentral.com/health/ways-to-go-with-the-flow-and-stay-in-the-moment#:~:text=Practice%20mindfulness

DeVencentis, P. (2018, September 12). William Paterson University art professor's "Paper Money" painting in line for award. North Jersey Media Group. https://www.northjersey.com/story/news/passaic/wayne/2018/09/12/william-paterson-university-art-professor-zhiyuan-cong-paints-history-paper-money/1205471002/

Do You Know About The Zhou Dynasty? Trivia Quiz - Trivia & Questions. (n.d.). Www.proprofs.com. Retrieved July 5, 2024, from https://www.proprofs.com/quiz-school/story.php?title=62-quiz--zhou-dynasty-new-ideas

Donn, L. (n.d.). Clothing in Ancient China - Ancient China for Kids. China.mrdonn.org. https://china.mrdonn.org/clothing.html#:~:text=People%20in%20ancient%20China%20wore

Douglas, C. (n.d.). Quizizz — The world's most engaging learning platform. Quizizz.com. Retrieved July 17, 2024, from https://quizizz.com/admin/quiz/5f828cbd26f122001bb1b354/ancient-chinese-inventions?fromSearch=true&source=

Ducksters. (2018). Kids History: The Song Dynasty of Ancient China. Ducksters.com. https://www.ducksters.com/history/china/song_dynasty.php

Ducksters. (2019a). Ancient China: Shang Dynasty. Ducksters.com. https://www.ducksters.com/history/china/shang_dynasty.php

Ducksters. (2019b). Kids History: Festivals in Ancient China. Ducksters.com. https://www.ducksters.com/history/china/chinese_festivals.php

Ducksters. (2019c). Kids History: The Zhou Dynasty of Ancient China. Ducksters.com. https://www.ducksters.com/history/china/zhou_dynasty.php

E., K. (n.d.). The Zhou Dynasty | 116 plays | Quizizz. Quizizz.com. Retrieved July 4, 2024, from https://quizizz.com/admin/quiz/5c6c0ff0217d20001bf1fda5/the-zhou-dynasty

Early Trans-Oceanic Trade In South and Southeast Asia | Silk Roads Programme. (n.d.). En.unesco.org. Retrieved July 23, 2024, from https://en.unesco.org/silkroad/knowledge-bank/early-trans-oceanic-trade-south-and-southeast-asia#:~:text=Buddhist%20monasteries%20were%20established%20close

Economic. (n.d.). Shang Dynasty. https://www.shangdynasty.info/economic#:~:text=Shang%20economy%20had%20three%20main

ECONOMY. (n.d.). YuaN DynastY. https://shaiyasmntha.wixsite.com/m3sit3/economy#:~:text=Under%20the%20wise%20governing%20the

Economy. (n.d.). Tang China. https://huntertangdynasty.weebly.com/economy.html#:~:text=In%20the%20Tang%20dynasty%2C%20the

Editors, H. com. (2017, December 21). Han Dynasty - Dates, Rulers & Legacy. HISTORY. https://www.history.com/topics/ancient-china/han-dynasty#silk-road

Eliza. (2022). How did Marco Polo's travels influence European culture? Tutorchase.com. https://www.tutorchase.com/answers/ib/history/how-did-marco-polo-s-travels-influence-european-culture

Endicott-West, E. (1994). The Yüan government and society (D. C. Twitchett & H. Franke, Eds.). Cambridge University Press; Cambridge University Press. https://www.cambridge.org/core/books/abs/cambridge-history-of-china/yuan-government-and-society/4D2947564A6DEFC71F9C01603D7AD3C3

ESCOBAR, M. (2024, June 2). Practices to Purify the Three Poisons of Buddhism. Lion's Roar. https://www.lionsroar.com/practices-to-purify-three-poisons/#:~:text=Greed%2C%20or%20craving%2C%20is%20rooted

Fei, J., & Pei, Q. (2019). Ferdinand von Richthofen's loess research in China. Progress in Physical Geography: Earth and Environment, 43(1), 144–156. https://doi.org/10.1177/0309133318824201

Fercility Jiang. (2019). Ancient Chinese Marriage Customs. China Highlights. https://www.chinahighlights.com/travelguide/culture/ancient-chinese-marriage-customs.htm

Feudalism in Ancient China: Lesson for Kids. (2022). Study.com. https://study.com/academy/lesson/feudalism-in-ancient-china-lesson-for-kids.html#:~:text=In%20ancient%20China%2C%20feudalism%20divided

Flores, M. (2023, December 4). The Principles of Taoism: Simplicity, Spontaneity, and Non-Action. Medium. https://medium.com/@mystic.flores/the-principles-of-taoism-simplicity-spontaneity-and-non-action-8e8849dc9b74#:~:text=Simplicity%2C%20or%20ziran%2C%20means%20being

Four Class System of China Yuan Dynasty. (2019). Travelchinaguide.com. https://www.travelchinaguide.com/intro/history/yuan/four-class-system.htm

Fronsdal, G. (n.d.). Buddhism in Nature – Insight Meditation Center. Insight Meditation Center. https://www.insightmeditationcenter.org/books-articles/buddhism-in-nature/#:~:text=A%20long%20tradition%20in%20Buddhism

Gardner, D. K. (2010, October 1). What Confucius says is useful to China's rulers. Los Angeles Times. https://www.latimes.com/archives/la-xpm-2010-oct-01-la-oe-gardner-confucius-20101001-story.html#:~:text=The%20ideal%20ruler%20embodies%20virtue

Gautama Buddha Quotes (Author of The Teaching of Buddha). (2018). Goodreads.com. https://www.goodreads.com/author/quotes/2167493.Gautama_Buddha

Gillan, J. (2019, September 9). Ancient Chinese Earthquake Detector Invented 2,000 Years Ago Really Worked! Ancient Origins Reconstructing the Story of Humanity's Past. https://www.ancient-origins.net/ancient-technology/incredible-earthquake-detector-invented-nearly-2000-years-ago-001377#google_vignette

Gotti, Z. (2024, March 24). The 5 Constant Virtues Of Life. Www.linkedin.com. https://www.linkedin.com/pulse/5-constant-virtues-life-zo%C3%A9-gotti-d3epf/

Great Wall of China Architecture | ArchitectureCourses.org. (n.d.). Www.architecturecourses.org. https://www.architecturecourses.org/learn/great-wall-china-architecture#:~:text=Great%20Wall%20of%20China%20Architecture%20Style&text=The%20style%20varies%20depending%20on

Great Wall, S. (n.d.). 10 Things to Know about the Great Wall of China. Google Arts & Culture. https://artsandculture.google.com/story/10-things-to-know-about-the-great-wall-of-china-simatai-great-wall-tourist-area/8wXxFCy7pu2HWA?hl=en

Grey, O. (2022, November 30). The Ming Treasure Voyages Spread Chinese Influence Throughout the World. Explorethearchive.com. https://explorethearchive.com/ming-treasure-voyages

Han Dynasty | 149 plays | Quizizz. (n.d.). Quizizz.com. Retrieved July 8, 2024, from https://quizizz.com/admin/quiz/5abcd140a19a1b0019723b00/han-dynasty

Han Dynasty Social Structure - The Han Society & Classes. (2014). Thehandynasty.com. https://thehandynasty.com/han-dynasty-social-structure.html

Handle-shaped blade | China | Western Zhou dynasty (1046–771 BCE). (n.d.). The Metropolitan Museum of Art. Retrieved July 8, 2024, from https://www.metmuseum.org/art/collection/search/44783#:~:text=Throughout%20the%20Shang%20and%20Zhou

Harvard Art Museums. (n.d.). Harvardartmuseums.org. https://harvardartmuseums.org/tour/497/slide/11107

Heavenly horses - legend of the origin. (n.d.). Www.advantour.com. https://www.advantour.com/uzbekistan/legends/heavenly-horses.htm#:~:text=Heavenly%20horses%20of%20Ferghana&text=These%20horses%20had%20great%20power

Heston, L. (n.d.). Zhou Dynasty Questions. Quizlet. Retrieved July 5, 2024, from https://quizlet.com/689058692/zhou-dynasty-questions-flash-cards/?isSignupSession

HISTORY.COM EDITORS. (2018, August 21). Shang Dynasty. HISTORY. https://www.history.com/topics/ancient-china/shang-dynasty

History.com Editors. (2017, November 3). Silk Road. History.com; A&E Television Networks. https://www.history.com/topics/ancient-middle-east/silk-road

Horwitz, T. (2021, June 15). TAO TE CHING BY LAO TZU - THE RULER. Cloud Hands Press. https://www.cloudhandspress.com/post/tao-te-ching-by-lao-tzu-the-ruler#:~:text=The%20ruler%20allows%20things%20to

How did trade along the Silk Road contribute to employment? (n.d.). Brainly. Retrieved July 21, 2024, from https://brainly.com/question/17908792

How the ancient Chinese used "oracle bones" to tell the future. (n.d.). History Skills. Retrieved July 3, 2024, from https://www.historyskills.com/classroom/year-7/oracle-bones/#:~:text=What%20kinds%20of%20questions%20were

How were Genghis and Kublai Khan alike? (n.d.). Study.com. Retrieved July 13, 2024, from https://homework.study.com/explanation/how-were-genghis-and-kublai-khan-alike.html#:~:text=Genghis%20Khan%20and%20Kublai%20Khan,Mongol%20Empire%20through%20military%20conquests.

Howard, M. (2022, October 31). Who invented toilet paper? Bumboo. https://www.bumboo.eco/blogs/news/who-invented-toilet-paper#:~:text=The%20Chinese%20Imperial%20Court%20of

https://taiwantoday.tw/news.php?unit=&post=. (1968, March 1). Taiwan Today. https://taiwantoday.tw/news.php?unit=20

Hurry, A. (n.d.). Kublai Khan | Biography, Accomplishments & Facts. Study.com. Retrieved July 15, 2024, from https://study.com/learn/lesson/kublai-khan-facts-accomplishments.html#:~:text=The%20grandson%20of%20the%20infamous,he%20had%20betrayed%20Mongol%20traditions.

Imperial China's Dynasties. (n.d.). Education.nationalgeographic.org. https://education.nationalgeographic.org/resource/imperial-chinas-dynasties/6th-grade/

Introduction- Beijing Ancient Observatory- The Beijing Planetarium. (2024). Bjp.org.cn. https://www.bjp.org.cn/en/Beijing%20Ancient%20Observatory/Introduction/index.shtml

Jacksonville, F. S. C. at. (n.d.). Daoism. Fscj.pressbooks.pub. https://fscj.pressbooks.pub/worldreligions/chapter/daoism/#:~:text=There%20are%20no%20%E2%80%9Cbad%20people

Jamie Carter. (2021, May 25). Chinese astronomy: a guide to ancient stargazing in China. Www.skyatnightmagazine.com. https://www.skyatnightmagazine.com/space-science/chinese-astronomy

Jaroff, L. (1997, March 17). CRAZY ABOUT COMETS. TIME. https://time.com/archive/6730507/crazy-about-comets/

Kallie Szczepanski. (2018). Four Principles to China's Mandate of Heaven. ThoughtCo. https://www.thoughtco.com/the-mandate-of-heaven-195113

Kane, M., & Sundstrom, A. (n.d.). Ancient Chinese Inventions and Discoveries | Quizizz. Quizizz.com. Retrieved July 18, 2024, from https://quizizz.com/admin/quiz/65dca3f0e193b20d15ed0c4b/ancient-chinese-inventions-and-discoveries?fromSearch=true&source=

Kauffman, D. (n.d.). Shang Dynasty Quiz | Quizizz. Quizizz.com. Retrieved July 4, 2024, from https://quizizz.com/admin/quiz/5e6bbdd53a9611001d0fe47e?source=auto-trial-start&searchLocale=

Kelley, J. (2020, January 15). A brief history of Calligraphy. HowJoyful. https://www.howjoyful.com/calligraphy-history/#:~:text=The%20origin%20of%20Calligraphy%20with

Keown, D. (2015, October 12). Top ten facts about Buddhism | OUPblog. OUPblog. https://blog.oup.com/2015/09/10-facts-about-buddhism/

Khan Academy. (n.d.). Zheng He (article). Khan Academy. https://www.khanacademy.org/humanities/big-history-project/expansion-interconnection/exploration-interconnection/a/zheng-he

Khan Academy. (2008). Rise of Chinese Dynasties. Khan Academy. https://www.khanacademy.org/humanities/world-history/ancient-medieval/zhou-qin-han-china/a/rise-of-chinese-dynasties

Kids History: Civil Service in Ancient China. (n.d.). Www.ducksters.com. https://www.ducksters.com/history/china/civil_service_government.php#:~:text=The%20civil%20service%20was%20started

Kids History: Forbidden City of Ancient China. (n.d.). Www.ducksters.com. Retrieved July 27, 2024, from https://www.ducksters.com/history/china/forbidden_city.php#:~:text=The%20Forbidden%20City%20also%20served

Kids History: The Legend of Silk in Ancient China. (n.d.). Www.ducksters.com. https://www.ducksters.com/history/china/legend_of_silk.php#:~:text=Keeping%20Silk%20a%20Secret&text=Nobles%20and%20kings%20of%20foreign

Kids History: The Tang Dynasty of Ancient China. (2019). Ducksters.com. https://www.ducksters.com/history/china/tang_dynasty.php

King Tang (Chinese and Japanese) | Grinnell College's Liberal Arts Club Band. (n.d.). GRINNELL COLLEGE'S LIBERAL ARTS CLUB BAND. https://liberalartsclubband.sites.grinnell.edu/annotations/h-o/king-tang-chinese/#:~:text=King%20Tang%20(Chinese%20and%20Japanese%2Fd.

Kublai Khan. (n.d.). Education.nationalgeographic.org. https://education.nationalgeographic.org/resource/kublai-khan/

Kublai Khan | World Civilization. (n.d.). Courses.lumenlearning.com. Retrieved July 14, 2024, from https://courses.lumenlearning.com/suny-hccc-worldcivilization/chapter/kublai-khan/#:~:text=At%20the%20time%20of%20Kublai

Kunzli, B. (2023, July 17). Embracing Simplicity: The Path of Living Simply. Medium. https://medium.com/@kunzlibirgit/embracing-simplicity-the-path-of-living-simply-2dbee1515f5f#:~:text=Simplicity%20in%20Buddhism%3A%20Buddhism%20teaches

Laboratory, N. H. M. F. (n.d.). Early Chinese Compass – 400 BC - Magnet Academy. Nationalmaglab.org. https://nationalmaglab.org/magnet-academy/history-of-electricity-magnetism/museum/early-chinese-compass-400-bc/#:~:text=People%20usually%20built%20early%20compasses

Lachman, C. (n.d.). Chinese Calligraphy. Asia Society. https://asiasociety.org/education/chinese-calligraphy#:~:text=In%20China%2C%20from%20a%20very

Lai, S., & Brown, W. T. (2006, November). FSI | SPICE - The Shang Dynasty, 1600 to 1050 BCE. Spice.fsi.stanford.edu.

https://spice.fsi.stanford.edu/docs/the_shang_dynasty_1600_to_1050_bce#:~:text=The%20Shang%20made%20many%20contributions

Landscape Painting in Chinese Art. (2022). Metmuseum.org. https://www.metmuseum.org/toah/hd/clpg/hd_clpg.htm#:~:text=By%20the%20late%20Tang%20dynasty

Legal Rights Of Chinese Women In The 17th Century Ming Dynasty | Cram. (n.d.). Www.cram.com. https://www.cram.com/essay/Legal-Rights-Of-Chinese-Women-In-The/PKDR4H9CX5W#:~:text=Throughout%20ancient%20China%20and%20continuing

Leung, I. (2008, August). Early Writing Technologies. Asia Society. https://asiasociety.org/education/writing-and-technology-china#:~:text=These%20bamboo%20or%20wood%20documents,sixth%20or%20seventh%20century%20B.C.E.

Linton, B. (2024, January 10). The Significance of Self-Reflection in Zen Buddhism: Insights from Zen Master Dogen. Medium. https://brucelinton.medium.com/the-significance-of-self-reflection-in-zen-buddhism-insights-from-zen-master-dogen-fcd6f7571ae3

Low, K. (2013). Materialism, Confucianism and Confucian Values. Educational Research, 4(5), 403–412. https://www.interesjournals.org/articles/materialism-confucianism-and-confucian-values.pdf

Low, K. C. P. (2013). Confucian Ethics. Encyclopedia of Corporate Social Responsibility, 437–443. https://doi.org/10.1007/978-3-642-28036-8_594

Lumen Learning. (2008). Culture Under the Song Dynasty | World Civilization. Lumenlearning.com. https://courses.lumenlearning.com/suny-hccc-worldcivilization/chapter/culture-under-the-song-dynasty/

Luo, S. (2019). Happiness and the Good Life: A Classical Confucian Perspective. Dao, 18(1), 41–58. https://doi.org/10.1007/s11712-018-9640-8

Lyn, V. (2021, March 1). HUMAN BEINGS – ARE WE BORN GOOD OR EVIL? Medium. https://vincentlyn.medium.com/human-beings-are-we-born-good-or-evil-4dca3e19b82f#:~:text=Whether%20humans%20are%20born%20good

Mack, L. (2019, August 15). Filial Piety: An Important Chinese Cultural Value. ThoughtCo. https://www.thoughtco.com/filial-piety-in-chinese-688386

Mahadane, R. (2019, November 1). The Philosophy Of Flow — Taoism. Medium. https://medium.com/novasemita/the-philosophy-of-flow-taoism-f176f1de2999

Mañé, A. (2021, December 1). Zheng He and the Era of the Great Chinese Maritime Expeditions. European Guanxi.

https://www.europeanguanxi.com/post/zheng-he-and-the-era-of-the-great-chinese-maritime-expeditions#:~:text=Zh%C3%A8ng%20H%C3%A9

Marco Polo – Silk Road Traveler and Explorer. (2016). Travelchinaguide.com. https://www.travelchinaguide.com/silk-road/history/traveler-marco-polo.htm

Mark, E. (2015, August 22). Great Wall of China. World History Encyclopedia. https://www.worldhistory.org/Great_Wall_of_China/

Mark, E. (2016a, January 10). Xia Dynasty. World History Encyclopedia. https://www.worldhistory.org/Xia_Dynasty/#google_vignette

Mark, E. (2016b, January 31). Legalism. World History Encyclopedia. https://www.worldhistory.org/Legalism/

Mark, E. (2016c, February 26). Oracle Bones. World History Encyclopedia. https://www.worldhistory.org/Oracle_Bones/

Mark, E. (2016d, February 28). Tang Dynasty. World History Encyclopedia. https://www.worldhistory.org/Tang_Dynasty/

Mark, E. (2016e, March 9). Emperor Taizong of Tang. World History Encyclopedia. https://www.worldhistory.org/Emperor_Taizong_of_Tang/

Mark, E. (2016f, April 21). Religion in Ancient China. World History Encyclopedia. https://www.worldhistory.org/article/891/religion-in-ancient-china/

Mark, E. (2016g, April 27). Daily Life in Ancient China. World History Encyclopedia. https://www.worldhistory.org/article/890/daily-life-in-ancient-china/

Mark, J. (2012a, December 18). Ancient China. World History Encyclopedia; World History Encyclopedia. https://www.worldhistory.org/china/

Mark, J. (2012b, December 18). Shi Huangdi. World History Encyclopedia. https://www.worldhistory.org/Shi_Huangdi/

Mark, J. (2020a, July 1). Zhou Dynasty. World History Encyclopedia. https://www.worldhistory.org/Zhou_Dynasty/

Mark, J. (2020b, July 3). Han Dynasty. World History Encyclopedia. https://www.worldhistory.org/Han_Dynasty/

Mark, J. (2020c, July 9). Lao-Tzu. World History Encyclopedia. https://www.worldhistory.org/Lao-Tzu/

Mark, J. J. (2020a, July 1). Qin Dynasty. World History Encyclopedia. https://www.worldhistory.org/Qin_Dynasty/

Mark, J. J. (2020b, July 9). Sun-Tzu. World History Encyclopedia. https://www.worldhistory.org/Sun-Tzu/#google_vignette

MarkWalkerFord. (2021, March 16). 10 Interesting Chinese Porcelain Facts. Rob Turner China Designs. https://robturner.co.uk/infographics/10-interesting-chinese-porcelain-facts/

Maser, M., & Jeffers, J. (n.d.). Zhou Dynasty | Quizizz. Quizizz.com. Retrieved July 5, 2024, from https://quizizz.com/admin/quiz/620c5892cc10e6001d7767ea/zhou-dynasty?fromSearch=true&source=

May, T. (2008). The Mongol Empire in World History. World History Connected, 5(2). https://worldhistoryconnected.press.uillinois.edu/5.2/may.html#:~:text=World%20History%20and%20the%20Mongols

michel. (2023, September 14). Genghis Khan. How the Mongols changed the world - Society of Friends of the Cernuschi Museum. Société Des Amis Du Musée Cernuschi. https://amis-musee-cernuschi.org/en/gengis-khan-comment-les-mongols-ont-change-le-monde/#:~:text=After%20years%20of%20violent%20conquests

Milligan, M. (2022, October 17). Liu Bang – The peasant that become an Emperor. HeritageDaily - Archaeology News. https://www.heritagedaily.com/2022/10/liu-bang-the-peasant-that-become-an-emperor/145001

Ming Dynasty Social Structure - The Ming Society & Classes. (2014). Themingdynasty.org. https://themingdynasty.org/ming-dynasty-social-structure.html

Ming Tombs. (n.d.). English.beijing.gov.cn. Retrieved July 26, 2024, from https://english.beijing.gov.cn/beijinginfo/culture/culturaltreasures/sevenculture/202401/t20240111_3532654.html#:~:text=Established%20in%201409%2C%20these%20tombs

Mongol Empire. (n.d.). Britannica Kids. Retrieved July 13, 2024, from https://kids.britannica.com/students/article/Mongol-Empire/275900#:~:text=The%20Mongols%20were%20the%20first

Mongol empire - Effects of Mongol rule. (2019). In Encyclopædia Britannica. https://www.britannica.com/place/Mongol-empire/Effects-of-Mongol-rule

Mongols in World History | Asia for Educators. (n.d.-a). Afe.easia.columbia.edu. https://afe.easia.columbia.edu/mongols/pastoral/pastoral.htm#:~:text=Introduction

Mongols in World History | Asia for Educators. (n.d.-b). Afe.easia.columbia.edu. https://afe.easia.columbia.edu/mongols/china/china3_a.htm

Mostafa. (2023, March 21). Battle Of Muye. Medium. https://medium.com/@mo2men.org.net/battle-of-muye-544e1eb02057

Mr. Lee. (n.d.). Chinese Inventions | Quizizz. Quizizz.com. Retrieved July 17, 2024, from https://quizizz.com/admin/quiz/6153487e0646b7001d810477/chinese-inventions?fromSearch=true&source=

Multiple Choice Quiz. (n.d.). Oxford University Press. Retrieved July 4, 2024, from https://global.oup.com/us/companion.websites/9780195332872/student/chapter4/quiz/

Museum, S. (n.d.). The Chinese compass and the birth of navigation. Google Arts & Culture. https://artsandculture.google.com/story/the-chinese-compass-and-the-birth-of-navigation-sichuan-museum/NwUh8_iOJNTQLw?hl=en

My China Roots. (n.d.). Euro-Travel-Example.com. https://www.mychinaroots.com/wiki/article/haijin

N.S. Gill. (2019). Was the Xia Dynasty of Ancient China Real or Mythical? ThoughtCo. https://www.thoughtco.com/xia-dynasty-117676

Nanji, A., & Niyozov, S. (2002). The Silk Road: Crossroads and Encounters of Faiths. Smithsonian Folklife Festival. https://festival.si.edu/2002/the-silk-road/the-silk-road-crossroads-and-encounters-of-faith/smithsonian#:~:text=The%20Silk%20Road%20provided%20a

Napthali, L. (2023, February 21). LibGuides: Ancient China: Everyday Life. Library.norwood.vic.edu.au. https://library.norwood.vic.edu.au/c.php?g=946985&p=6861428#:~:text=In%20ancient%20China%20the%20overwhelming

National Geographic. (2022, May 20). The Pax Mongolica | National Geographic Society. Education.nationalgeographic.org. https://education.nationalgeographic.org/resource/pax-mongolica/

National Geographic. (2023, October 19). Huang He Valley | National Geographic Society. Education.nationalgeographic.org. https://education.nationalgeographic.org/resource/huang-he-valley/

National Geographic Society. (2022a, May 20). Chinese Religions and Philosophies | National Geographic Society. Education.nationalgeographic.org; National Geographic Society. https://education.nationalgeographic.org/resource/chinese-religions-and-philosophies/

National Geographic Society. (2022b, May 20). The Silk Road. Education.nationalgeographic.org; National Geographic. https://education.nationalgeographic.org/resource/silk-road/

National Geographic Society. (2022c, October 27). The Art of War | National Geographic Society. Education.nationalgeographic.org. https://education.nationalgeographic.org/resource/art-war/

National Geographic Society. (2023a, October 19). Taoism. National Geographic. https://education.nationalgeographic.org/resource/taoism/

National Geographic Society. (2023b, November 2). Buddhism. Education.nationalgeographic.org; National Geographic.

https://education.nationalgeographic.org/resource/buddhism/

National Geographic Society. (2024, March 6). Confucianism. National Geographic; National Geographic Society. https://education.nationalgeographic.org/resource/confucianism/

National Museum of Asian Art, Smithsonian Institution. (n.d.). Zhou Dynasty (c. 1050–221 B.C.E.), an introduction – Smarthistory. Smarthistory.org. https://smarthistory.org/zhou-dynasty-intro/

Neo Confucianism: Definition, Beliefs & Influence | StudySmarter. (n.d.). StudySmarter UK. Retrieved July 27, 2024, from https://www.studysmarter.co.uk/explanations/history/modern-world-history/neo-confucianism/#:~:text=Key%20points%20demonstrating%20the%20impact

Ng, R. M.-C. (2009). College and Character: What Did Confucius Teach Us About The Importance of Integrating Ethics, Character, Learning, and Education? Journal of College and Character, 10(4). https://doi.org/10.2202/1940-1639.1045

Northwestern Medicine. (n.d.). Traditional Chinese Medicine. Northwestern Medicine. Retrieved July 23, 2024, from https://www.nm.org/conditions-and-care-areas/integrative-medicine/traditional-chinese-medicine#:~:text=Originating%20over%205%2C000%20years%20ago

Origins of the Song Dynasty | World Civilization. (n.d.). Courses.lumenlearning.com. Retrieved July 10, 2024, from https://courses.lumenlearning.com/suny-hccc-worldcivilization/chapter/origins-of-the-song-dynasty/#:~:text=using%20a%20compass.-

Pang, K. (2022, January 4). The Spring and Autumn Period: Emerge of the Confucianism. China Highlights. https://www.chinahighlights.com/travelguide/china-history/spring-and-autumn-period.htm

Patterns of Modern Chinese History. (n.d.). Oxford University Press. https://global.oup.com/us/companion.websites/9780199946457/stud/ch1/Q1/

Peng, Dr. Y. (n.d.). The Forbidden City (article) | China. Khan Academy. https://www.khanacademy.org/humanities/ap-art-history/south-east-se-asia/china-art/a/forbidden-city#:~:text=The%20Forbidden%20City%20was%20the

Ph. D., H., J. D., U. of W. S. of L., & B. A., H. (2019a, July 22). Why Did Ming China End the Treasure Fleet Voyages? ThoughtCo. https://www.thoughtco.com/why-did-the-treasure-fleet-stop-195223

Ph. D., H., J. D., U. of W. S. of L., & B. A., H. (2019b, October 16). How Kublai Khan and the Mongols Invaded Japan. ThoughtCo. https://www.thoughtco.com/the-mongol-invasions-of-japan-195559#:~:text=The%20Mongol%20Invasions%20of%20Japan%20in%201274%20and%201281%20devastated

Pillalamarri, A. (2016, August 9). Revealed: The Truth About China's Legendary Xia Dynasty. Thediplomat.com. https://thediplomat.com/2016/08/revealed-the-truth-about-chinas-legendary-xia-dynasty/

Pimentel, N. (n.d.). The Silk Road | Quizizz. Quizizz.com. Retrieved July 20, 2024, from https://quizizz.com/admin/quiz/5ec7746d3c0bbd001bd1e890/the-silk-road

Png, J. (n.d.). Origins of Chinese Chess: Gen. Han Xin P.1. Xiangqi.com. Retrieved July 24, 2024, from https://www.xiangqi.com/articles/origins-of-xiangqi-chinese-chess-12-general-han-xin#:~:text=During%20the%20war%20to%20conquer

Poetics of Invention. (2024). Ou.edu. https://poeticsofinvention.ou.edu/rooms/imperial-exams#:~:text=The%20Chinese%20Imperial%20Examination%20System

Politics in China -Dynasties. (n.d.). Retrieved July 9, 2024, from https://mrtickler.weebly.com/uploads/5/4/3/8/54383485/fall_of_qin_dynasty_documents.pdf

Powell, E. (n.d.). Yuan Dynasty | 354 plays | Quizizz. Quizizz.com. Retrieved July 11, 2024, from https://quizizz.com/admin/quiz/5de19dba404fb7001c6585f8/yuan-dynasty?fromSearch=true&source=

primeo. (2022, October 6). Song Dynasty Architecture: Pagodas, Temples, Bridges & Tombs. Totally History. https://totallyhistory.com/song-dynasty-architecture/

Producing the Goods | Silk Roads Programme. (n.d.). En.unesco.org. https://en.unesco.org/silkroad/knowledge-bank/producing-goods

ProProfs Editorial Team . (n.d.). The Song Dynasty Quiz - Trivia & Questions. Www.proprofs.com. Retrieved July 10, 2024, from https://www.proprofs.com/quiz-school/story.php?title=song-dynasty-quiz

purl, C. (n.d.). xia dynasty | Quizizz. Quizizz.com. Retrieved July 4, 2024, from https://quizizz.com/admin/quiz/5c069768cedf27001adc89d8/xia-dynasty

Qin Dynasty | 82 plays | Quizizz. (n.d.). Quizizz.com. Retrieved July 8, 2024, from https://quizizz.com/admin/quiz/5db83eaef4e8f9001b2af3d8/qin-dynasty

Qin Dynasty | Definition, Ruler & Legalism. (n.d.). Study.com. Retrieved July 9, 2024, from https://study.com/academy/lesson/the-qin-dynasty-in-china-the-great-wall-legalism.html#:~:text=and%20educate%20themselves.-,The%20legalism%20philosophy%20influenced%20Qin%20Shi%20Huangdi's%20rule%20by%20creating,such%20as%20the%20Zhou%20Dynasty.

Quan, C. (2024, January 3). The Forbidden City — Citadel of China's Last 24 Emperors. China Highlights. https://www.chinahighlights.com/beijing/forbidden-city/

Quiz: Ancient China - The Silk Road. (n.d.). Www.ducksters.com. https://www.ducksters.com/history/china/silk_road_questions.php

Rathke, A. (n.d.). Chinese Pottery Traditions. https://www.uwlax.edu/globalassets/offices-services/urc/jur-online/pdf/2001/a_rathke.pdf

READ: Confucianism (article). (n.d.). Khan Academy. https://www.khanacademy.org/humanities/whp-origins/era-3-cities-societies-and-empires-6000-bce-to-700-c-e/35-development-of-belief-systems-betaa/a/read-confucianism-beta#:~:text=Confucius%20believed%20that%20to%20restore

READ: Daoism (article). (n.d.). Khan Academy. https://www.khanacademy.org/humanities/whp-origins/era-3-cities-societies-and-empires-6000-bce-to-700-c-e/35-development-of-belief-systems-betaa/a/read-daoism-beta#:~:text=The%20Daoist%20community%20believes%20that

READ: Daoism (article) | Khan Academy. (2023). Khan Academy. https://www.khanacademy.org/humanities/whp-origins/era-3-cities-societies-and-empires-6000-bce-to-700-c-e/35-development-of-belief-systems-betaa/a/read-daoism-beta#:~:text=Daoists%20consider%20a%20Confucian%20emphasis

READ: Zhou and Qin Dynasty — China (article). (n.d.). Khan Academy. https://www.khanacademy.org/humanities/whp-origins/era-3-cities-societies-and-empires-6000-bce-to-700-c-e/36-the-growth-of-empires-betaa/a/read-zhou-and-qin-dynasty-china-beta#:~:text=China%20became%20increasingly%20chaotic%20as

Riley, A. (n.d.). The Silk Road | 8K plays | Quizizz. Quizizz.com. Retrieved July 20, 2024, from https://quizizz.com/admin/quiz/5ace60b2ab981b001bd8ddc1/the-silk-road

Rise of the Tang Dynasty | World Civilization. (2019). Lumenlearning.com. https://courses.lumenlearning.com/suny-hccc-worldcivilization/chapter/rise-of-the-tang-dynasty/

Rosemary. (2019, July 7). The History of Woodblock Printing. WNY Book Arts Center. https://wnybookarts.org/the-history-of-woodblock-printing/#:~:text=Well%2C%20the%20invention%20of%20woodblock

Samie, W. (2021, October 16). Xia Dynasty: The First of the Chinese Dynasties. TheCollector. https://www.thecollector.com/xia-dynasty-first-ancient-chinese-dynasty/

Segall, S. Z. (2024). Buddhism and Western Psychology. St Andrews Encyclopaedia of Theology. https://www.saet.ac.uk/Buddhism/BuddhismandWesternPsychology#:~:text=Despite%20these%20differences%20in%20vision

Seismology in Ancient China | Encyclopedia.com. (n.d.).
Www.encyclopedia.com. https://www.encyclopedia.com/science/encyclopedias-almanacs-transcripts-and-maps/seismology-ancient-china#:~:text=Little%20wonder%2C%20then%20that%20scientists

Shades of Blue: Subtle Differences in Chinese Blue-and-White Porcelain. (2019, February 4). Christies.com; Christie's. https://www.christies.com/en/stories/shades-of-blue-subtle-differences-in-chinese-blue-and-white-porcelain-775ffe5d69b54ed08e65ac8a625a1287

Shan, J. (2020, February 3). What Do Yin and Yang Represent? ThoughtCo. https://www.thoughtco.com/yin-and-yang-629214

Shang Dynasty | 399 plays | Quizizz. (n.d.). Quizizz.com. Retrieved July 4, 2024, from https://quizizz.com/admin/quiz/5891e16b801a1505270fe310/shang-dynasty

Shang Dynasty civilization (article). (n.d.). Khan Academy. https://www.khanacademy.org/humanities/world-history/world-history-beginnings/shang-dynasty-china/a/shang-dynasty-article#:~:text=Bronze%20swords%20and%20spearheads%20were

Shang Dynasty Ritual Bronze Vessels. (2016). Khan Academy. https://www.khanacademy.org/humanities/art-asia/imperial-china/shang-dynasty/a/shang-dynasty-ritual-bronze-vessels

Shaw, S. (n.d.). Quizizz — The world's most engaging learning platform. Quizizz.com. Retrieved July 11, 2024, from https://quizizz.com/admin/quiz/5c104a0d734fb5001a351438/yuan-dynasty?fromSearch=true&source=

Shears, E. (2023, December 6). The Splendid Artistry of Ancient Xia Dynasty Pottery – Artabys. Artabys. https://artabys.com/the-splendid-artistry-of-ancient-xia-dynasty-pottery/#:~:text=Xia%20dynasty%20pottery%20(2070%2D1600

Silk Road Worksheet. (n.d.). Retrieved July 20, 2024, from https://www.cloverleaflocal.org/Downloads/Silk%20Road%20Worksheet.pdf

Singh Kalakoti, V. (n.d.). Finding Flow State: The Wisdom of Taoism. Www.linkedin.com. https://www.linkedin.com/pulse/finding-flow-state-wisdom-taoism-vivek-singh-kalakoti/

Singh, S. (2023, October 30). The Mongol Empire: Kublai Khan's Impact on China. Owlcation. https://owlcation.com/humanities/The-Mongols-Kublai-Khans-Impact-on-China#:~:text=He%20reformed%20China

Smith, S. (2023). Top 10 facts about the Terracotta Warriors. National Museums Liverpool; Scott Smith. https://www.liverpoolmuseums.org.uk/stories/top-10-facts-about-terracotta-warriors

Smithsonian's National Museum of Asian Art. (n.d.). Yuan dynasty, an introduction (article). Khan Academy. https://www.khanacademy.org/humanities/art-asia/imperial-china/yuan-dynasty/a/yuan-dynasty-an-introduction#:~:text=They%20abandoned%20naturalism%20in%20favor

Society Under the Zhou Dynasty | World Civilization. (n.d.). Courses.lumenlearning.com. https://courses.lumenlearning.com/suny-hccc-worldcivilization/chapter/society-under-the-zhou-dynasty/#:~:text=Delegating%20regional%20control%20in%20this

Song Dynasty (960-1279): Chinese History, Art & Facts. (2024, March 5). GeeksforGeeks. https://www.geeksforgeeks.org/song-dynasty-960-1279/

Song Dynasty Established in China. (n.d.). Education.nationalgeographic.org. https://education.nationalgeographic.org/resource/song-dynasty-established-china/

Song, C. (2014). Silk Road Facts — 12 Things You Should Know. China Highlights. https://www.chinahighlights.com/silkroad/silkroad-facts.htm

Stokes Brown, C. (n.d.). Marco Polo (article). Khan Academy. https://www.khanacademy.org/humanities/big-history-project/expansion-interconnection/exploration-interconnection/a/marco-polo

Szczepanski, K. (n.d.-a). Learn More About China's Mythical 3 Sovereigns and 5 Emperors. ThoughtCo. https://www.thoughtco.com/chinas-three-sovereigns-and-five-emperors-195258#:~:text=Again%20according%20to%20Sima%20Qian

Szczepanski, K. (n.d.-b). Zheng He's Huge Treasure Ships. ThoughtCo. https://www.thoughtco.com/zheng-hes-treasure-ships-195235#:~:text=Incredibly%2C%20the%20largest%20ships%20in

Szczepanski, K. (2013, May 22). Effects of the Mongol Empire on Europe. ThoughtCo; ThoughtCo. https://www.thoughtco.com/mongols-effect-on-europe-195621

Tang And Song Dynasties Quiz - Trivia & Questions. (n.d.). Www.proprofs.com. Retrieved July 9, 2024, from https://www.proprofs.com/quiz-school/story.php?title=3dq-tang-and-song-dynasty-quiz

tang dynasty. (n.d.). Https://Quizlet.com/. Retrieved July 10, 2024, from https://quizlet.com/11577383/tang-dynasty-flash-cards/

Tang Dynasty | Quizizz. (n.d.). Quizizz.com. Retrieved July 9, 2024, from https://quizizz.com/admin/quiz/58bf3db32f772c1d1826ec0d/tang-dynasty

Tang, C. (2019). Yu Yuan — a Garden Oasis in the Center of Shanghai's Old City. China Highlights. https://www.chinahighlights.com/shanghai/attraction/yuyuan-garden.htm

Tavor, O. (n.d.). Ancestor Worship. Obo. https://www.oxfordbibliographies.com/display/document/obo-9780199920082/obo-9780199920082-0171.xml#:~:text=Ancestor%20worship%20refers%20to%20rituals

Team, D. (2023, July 27). Confucian Principles in Chinese Painting: Beginner's Guide. Daisie Blog. https://blog.daisie.com/confucian-principles-in-chinese-painting-beginners-guide/#:~:text=Confucianism%20considers%20art%20as%20a

Terry, W. (2021, April 25). What Is Karma, Really? Yoga Journal. https://www.yogajournal.com/yoga-101/what-is-karma-really/

Thagard , P. (2013, July 11). Karma—What Goes Around Comes Around? | Psychology Today. Www.psychologytoday.com. https://www.psychologytoday.com/intl/blog/hot-thought/201307/karma-what-goes-around-comes-around

The British Museum. (n.d.). Imperial China, an introduction – Smarthistory. Smarthistory.org. https://smarthistory.org/imperial-china-an-introduction/

The concept of Dhamma (Dharma) - Dhamma in Buddhism - GCSE Religious Studies Revision - AQA. (n.d.). BBC Bitesize. https://www.bbc.co.uk/bitesize/guides/zr7ck2p/revision/1#:~:text=Dhamma%20means%20

The Eastern Zhou Period | World Civilization. (n.d.). Courses.lumenlearning.com. https://courses.lumenlearning.com/suny-hccc-worldcivilization/chapter/the-eastern-zhou-period/#:~:text=The%20Spring%20and%20Autumn%20Period%20of%20Eastern%20Zhou&text=This%20period%20lasted%20from%20about

The Editors of Encyclopedia Britannica. (2019). Forbidden City | History, Facts, & Map. In Encyclopædia Britannica. https://www.britannica.com/topic/Forbidden-City

The First Emperor of China Destroys Most Records of the Past Along with 460, or More, Scholars : History of Information. (n.d.). Www.historyofinformation.com. https://www.historyofinformation.com/detail.php?id=2491#:~:text=%22Qin%20Shi%20Huang%20burned%20the

The Han Dynasty | 193 plays | Quizizz. (n.d.). Quizizz.com. Retrieved July 8, 2024, from https://quizizz.com/admin/quiz/5e32f9f022c7ab001ba973e4/the-han-dynasty

The Mandate of Heaven | World Civilization. (n.d.). Courses.lumenlearning.com. https://courses.lumenlearning.com/suny-hccc-worldcivilization/chapter/the-mandate-of-heaven/#:~:text=In%201046%20BCE%2C%20the%20Shang

The Metropolitan Museum of Art. (2019). Yuan Dynasty (1271–1368). Metmuseum.org. https://www.metmuseum.org/toah/hd/yuan/hd_yuan.htm

The Ming Dynasty | 1.1K plays | Quizizz. (n.d.). Quizizz.com. Retrieved July 16, 2024, from https://quizizz.com/admin/quiz/5c017b6316ab1a001a5a003d/the-ming-dynasty

The Mongol Dynasty. (n.d.). Asia Society. https://asiasociety.org/education/mongol-dynasty#:~:text=Although%20Kublai%20Khan%20tried%20to

The Qin Dynasty | 883 plays | Quizizz. (n.d.). Quizizz.com. Retrieved July 9, 2024, from https://quizizz.com/admin/quiz/56afeb01e31f46a2055e97f8/the-qin-dynasty

The Qin Dynasty | World Civilization. (n.d.). Courses.lumenlearning.com. https://courses.lumenlearning.com/suny-hccc-worldcivilization/chapter/the-qin-dynasty/#:~:text=Collapse%20of%20the%20Qin%20Dynasty&text=The%20First%20Emperor

The Role Of The Great Wall In Protecting The Silk Road. (n.d.). FasterCapital. Retrieved July 21, 2024, from https://fastercapital.com/topics/the-role-of-the-great-wall-in-protecting-the-silk-road.html

The Song Dynasty in China | Asia for Educators. (n.d.-a). Afe.easia.columbia.edu. https://afe.easia.columbia.edu/songdynasty-module/econ-rev-commercial.html

The Song Dynasty in China | Asia for Educators. (n.d.-b). Afe.easia.columbia.edu. https://afe.easia.columbia.edu/songdynasty-module/confucian-neo.html#:~:text=The%20revived%20Confucianism%20of%20the

The Song Dynasty in China | Asia for Educators. (n.d.-c). Afe.easia.columbia.edu. https://afe.easia.columbia.edu/songdynasty-module/tech-gunpowder.html#:~:text=Technological%20Advances%20during%20the%20Song&text=Song%20military%20engineers%20found%20gunpowder

The Song Dynasty in China | Asia for Educators. (n.d.-d). Afe.easia.columbia.edu. https://afe.easia.columbia.edu/songdynasty-module/econ-rev-money.html

The Xia Dynasty | Early World Civilizations. (n.d.). Courses.lumenlearning.com. Retrieved July 3, 2024, from https://courses.lumenlearning.com/atd-herkimer-worldcivilization/chapter/the-xia-dynasty/#:~:text=Debate%20Over%20the%20Existence%20of

The Yuan Dynasty. (n.d.). Quizlet. Retrieved July 15, 2024, from https://quizlet.com/678087980/the-yuan-dynasty-flash-cards/

The Yuan Dynasty | Boundless World History. (n.d.).
Courses.lumenlearning.com. https://courses.lumenlearning.com/tc3-boundless-worldhistory/chapter/the-yuan-dynasty/

The Zhou Dynasty. (2016, May 11). Nettelhorst. https://nettelhorst.org/ourpages/auto/2016/5/11/46419989/The%20Zhou%20Dynasty.pdf

The Zhou Dynasty | World Civilizations I (HIS101) – Biel. (n.d.).
Courses.lumenlearning.com. Retrieved July 5, 2024, from https://courses.lumenlearning.com/suny-fmcc-boundless-worldhistory/chapter/the-zhou-dynasty/#:~:text=crossbow%3A%20A%20mechanised%20weapon%2C%20based

Theobald, U. (n.d.). Yuan Dynasty - Political System (www.chinaknowledge.de).
Www.chinaknowledge.de. http://www.chinaknowledge.de/History/Yuan/yuan-admin.html#:~:text=Each%20%22province%22%20was%20governed%20by

Theobald, U. (2016, March 19). Ming-Period Economy (www.chinaknowledge.de). Www.chinaknowledge.de. http://www.chinaknowledge.de/History/Ming/ming-econ.html#:~:text=The%20Ming%20government%20thus%20started

Theobald, U. (2018, September 25). Zhou Period Religion (www.chinaknowledge.de). Www.chinaknowledge.de. http://www.chinaknowledge.de/History/Zhou/zhou-religion.html

Things to Do in Quanzhou, UNESCO World Cultural Heritage City_ News_ 福建省人民政府门户网站. (2024, January 31). Www.fujian.gov.cn. https://www.fujian.gov.cn/english/news/202402/t20240207_6393886.htm#:~:text=Quanzhou%2C%20a%20coastal%20city%20in

Top 20 Ancient Chinese Inventions. (n.d.). In https://china.usc.edu/sites/default/files/forums/Chinese%20Inventions.pdf. https://china.usc.edu/sites/default/files/forums/Chinese%20Inventions.pdf

Trade and Currency under the Yuan | World Civilization. (n.d.).
Courses.lumenlearning.com. https://courses.lumenlearning.com/suny-hccc-worldcivilization/chapter/trade-and-currency-under-the-yuan/#:~:text=Kublai%20Khan%20promoted%20commercial%2C%20scientific

Trueblood, B. (n.d.). Zhou Dynasty (L2) | 99 plays | Quizizz. Quizizz.com.
Retrieved July 5, 2024, from https://quizizz.com/admin/quiz/5f4aa405636a38001bfa4f36/zhou-dynasty?fromSearch=true&source=

Ulrich Theobald. (2020). Song Empire Government, Administration, and Law (www.chinaknowledge.de). Chinaknowledge.de; Ulrich Theobald. http://www.chinaknowledge.de/History/Song/song-admin.html

UMBRELLA. (n.d.). YONG ZHEN. Retrieved July 24, 2024, from
https://www.tsw.com.tw/en/about-
as#:~:text=According%20to%20legend%2C%20the%20first

UNESCO. (n.d.). Did you know?: The Spread of Buddhism in South and
Southeast Asia through the Trade Routes | Silk Roads Programme.
En.unesco.org. https://en.unesco.org/silkroad/content/did-you-know-spread-
buddhism-south-and-southeast-asia-through-trade-routes

UNESCO - Kun Qu opera. (n.d.). Ich.unesco.org. Retrieved July 26, 2024, from
https://ich.unesco.org/en/RL/kun-qu-opera-
00004#:~:text=Kun%20Qu%20Opera%20developed%20under

van Schaik, S. (2016, July 12). What Goes Around Comes Around: Our Faith in
Karma. Yale University Press. https://yalebooks.yale.edu/2016/07/12/what-goes-
around-comes-around-our-faith-in-karma/#:~:text=The%20Buddha

Wang, C., & Madson, N. (2013). Confucius - an overview | ScienceDirect
Topics. Www.sciencedirect.com.
https://www.sciencedirect.com/topics/psychology/confucius#:~:text=Within%20C
onfucianism%20there%20are%20five

Wang, V. (2016, January 28). 10 Unique Chinese Expressions You Need To
Know. Culture Trip. https://theculturetrip.com/asia/china/articles/10-unique-
chinese-expressions-you-need-to-
know#:~:text=s%C3%A0o%20zh%C7%92u%20x%C4%ABng%20(%E6%89%AB
%E5%B8%9A%E6%98%9F)%3A%20%E2%80%9Cbroom%20star%E2%80%9D
&text=The%20long%2C%20trailing%20tail%20of

Watts, A., & Heidegger, M. (n.d.). Laozi Facts for Kids. Kids.kiddle.co.
https://kids.kiddle.co/Laozi

Webquest and test printout for Ancient China - Xia Dynasty quiz. Printer
friendly version. (n.d.). Www.ducksters.com. Retrieved July 4, 2024, from
https://www.ducksters.com/history/china/xia_dynasty_print.php

What are oracle bones? (n.d.). BBC Bitesize. Retrieved July 4, 2024, from
https://www.bbc.co.uk/bitesize/articles/zsm6qhv#z64f3j6

What are the characteristics of Song Dynasty paintings? | 5 Answers from
Research papers. (n.d.). SciSpace - Question. Retrieved July 10, 2024, from
https://typeset.io/questions/what-are-the-characteristics-of-song-dynasty-paintings-
1k1mvkaq17

What did the Zhou Dynasty trade? (n.d.). Study.com. Retrieved July 7, 2024,
from https://homework.study.com/explanation/what-did-the-zhou-dynasty-
trade.html#:~:text=The%20Zhou%20dynasty%20traded%20within,the%20earlies
t%20dynasties%20of%20China.

What does Buddhism teach about the environment? - The world - GCSE
Religious Studies Revision - WJEC. (n.d.). BBC Bitesize.

https://www.bbc.co.uk/bitesize/guides/zc9bh39/revision/3#:~:text=For%20many%20Buddhists%2C%20the%20guiding

What weapons were used in the Western Zhou Dynasty? (n.d.). Study.com. Retrieved July 8, 2024, from https://homework.study.com/explanation/what-weapons-were-used-in-the-western-zhou-dynasty.html#:~:text=The%20Western%20Zhou%20Dynasty%20(c,%2C%20shields%2C%20and%20war%20chariots.

Whipps, H. (2008, April 6). How Gunpowder Changed the World. Live Science; Live Science. https://www.livescience.com/7476-gunpowder-changed-world.html

Who did the Shang people pray to? (n.d.). BBC Bitesize. https://www.bbc.co.uk/bitesize/articles/zc6h2nb#z7w33j6

Why was the Han dynasty a golden age? (n.d.). Study.com. Retrieved July 8, 2024, from https://homework.study.com/explanation/why-was-the-han-dynasty-a-golden-age.html

Why was the Zhou Dynasty in China so long lived? (n.d.). Study.com. Retrieved July 6, 2024, from https://homework.study.com/explanation/why-was-the-zhou-dynasty-in-china-so-long-lived.html#:~:text=That%20these%20many%20periods%20amalgamated,to%20a%20%20degree%20of%20stability.

Yellow River | Facts, Location & History. (n.d.). Study.com. Retrieved July 4, 2024, from https://study.com/learn/lesson/yellow-river-location-facts.html#:~:text=The%20Yellow%20River%20has%20many,second%2Dlargest%20river%20in%20China.

yin and yang. (n.d.). Britannica Kids. https://kids.britannica.com/students/article/yin-and-yang/277845#:~:text=Yin%20and%20yang%20mean%20literally

YU Garden – A Must-see Attraction in Shanghai – G-MEO. (n.d.). Gmeo China. Retrieved July 26, 2024, from https://www.gmeochina.com/students/why-study-in-china/chinese-culture/yu-garden-a-must-see-attraction-in-shanghai/#:~:text=Yu%20Garden%20(Chinese%3A%20%E8%B1%AB%E5%9B%AD%20Y%C3%B9

yuan dynasty. (n.d.). Www.fordlibrarymuseum.gov. https://www.fordlibrarymuseum.gov/museum/exhibits/china_exhibit/yuan.htm#:~:text=The%20native%20people%20were%20relegated

Yuan dynasty, an introduction (article). (n.d.). Khan Academy. https://www.khanacademy.org/humanities/art-asia/imperial-china/yuan-dynasty/a/yuan-dynasty-an-introduction#:~:text=Landscape%20painting%20became%20unprecedentedly%20popular

Yuan Dynasty and Kublai Khan Quiz. (n.d.). Quizgecko.com. Retrieved July 15, 2024, from https://quizgecko.com/learn/yuan-dynasty-and-kublai-khan-quiz-wgfrrk

Yuan Dynasty History. (n.d.). Quizgecko.com. Retrieved July 15, 2024, from https://quizgecko.com/learn/yuan-dynasty-history-xszcey

Yun, L. (2021, December 30). Bi Sheng, the Inventor of Movable Type-Experts in China-EnglishChannel. M.stdaily.com. http://m.stdaily.com/English/Service/2021-12/30/content_1243122.shtml

Yuting, S. (2019, May 21). Taoism emphasizes harmony between humanity and nature. News.cgtn.com. https://news.cgtn.com/news/3d3d674d7a45444f34457a6333566d54/index.html

Yuyuan Garden Shanghai, Yuyuan Garden Guide. (n.d.). Www.visitourchina.com. https://www.visitourchina.com/shanghai/attraction/yuyuan-garden.html

Zaju | Chinese theatre. (n.d.). Encyclopedia Britannica. https://www.britannica.com/art/zaju

Zheng, N. (n.d.). Chinese Traditional Etiquette Customs. Www.chinaculturetour.com. Retrieved July 25, 2024, from https://www.chinaculturetour.com/culture/etiquette-customs.htm#:~:text=Beginning%20in%20the%20Western%20Dynasty

Zhengkun, G. (n.d.). Dao De Jing and Western Science. FutureLearn. https://www.futurelearn.com/info/courses/taoism-and-western-culture/0/steps/84284#:~:text=Taoist%20alchemy%20paved%20the%20way

Zhihua Temple | Attractions. (n.d.). Lonely Planet. Retrieved July 26, 2024, from https://www.lonelyplanet.com/china/beijing/forbidden-city-and-dongcheng-central/attractions/zhihua-temple/a/poi-sig/368867/1333763

Zhou Dynasty & the Mandate of Heaven. (n.d.). Study.com. Retrieved July 7, 2024, from https://study.com/academy/lesson/zhou-dynasty-government-economy.html#:~:text=The%20Zhou%20Dynasty%20ended%20when,the%20confidence%20of%20its%20people.

周冰. (n.d.). Experts find more from Xia Dynasty dig. Www.chinadaily.com.cn. Retrieved July 4, 2024, from https://www.chinadaily.com.cn/a/202312/28/WS658cc841a31040ac301a9e07.html#:~:text=The%20remains%20of%20a%20palace

Zuñiga, E. (n.d.). Ancient China: Daily life | Quizizz. Quizizz.com. Retrieved July 17, 2024, from https://quizizz.com/admin/quiz/5eb46cfdb74f26001be23897/ancient-china-daily-life

Image References

[1] *BrokenSphere, CC BY 3.0 <https://creativecommons.org/licenses/by/3.0>, via Wikimedia Commons: https://commons.wikimedia.org/wiki/File:Mid_Shang_wine_vessel_SM.JPG*

[2] *Gary Todd, CC0, via Wikimedia Commons: https://commons.wikimedia.org/wiki/File:Shang_Chariot_Burial_20.jpg*

[3] *https://commons.wikimedia.org/wiki/File:King_Tang_of_Shang.jpg*

[4] *Gary Todd, CC0, via Wikimedia Commons: https://commons.wikimedia.org/wiki/File:Ancient_Chinese_Writing_on_Ox_Scapula,_Shang_Dynasty_Oracle_Bone,_Yinxu.jpg*

[5] *Gary Lee Todd, CC BY-SA 4.0 <https://creativecommons.org/licenses/by-sa/4.0>, via Wikimedia Commons: https://commons.wikimedia.org/wiki/File:Xia_Dynasty_pottery_jar.jpg*

[6] *Gary Todd from Xinzheng, China, CC0, via Wikimedia Commons: https://commons.wikimedia.org/wiki/File:Shang_Bronze_Helmet_(30762857384).jpg*

[7] *Gary Todd, CC0, via Wikimedia Commons: https://commons.wikimedia.org/wiki/File:Shang_Bone_Artifacts,_Spearheads,_Harpoon,_etc.jpg*

[8] *Gary Lee Todd, Ph.D., CC0, via Wikimedia Commons: https://commons.wikimedia.org/wiki/File:Shang_Jade_Ring_01.jpg*

[9] *Gary Lee Todd, Ph.D., CC0, via Wikimedia Commons: https://commons.wikimedia.org/wiki/File:006_Xia_or_Shang_Stone_Cowrie_Money.jpg*

[10] *fading, CC BY-SA 3.0 <https://creativecommons.org/licenses/by-sa/3.0>, via Wikimedia Commons: https://commons.wikimedia.org/wiki/File:Yellow_River_-_panoramio.jpg*

[11] *https://commons.wikimedia.org/wiki/File:King_Wu_of_Zhou_Dynasty.jpg*

[12] *Gary Todd from Xinzheng, China, CC0, via Wikimedia Commons: https://commons.wikimedia.org/wiki/File:Northern_Zhou_Ancient_Chinese_Coins_(15872675100).jpg*

[13] *Gary Todd from Xinzheng, China, CC0, via Wikimedia Commons:*
https://commons.wikimedia.org/wiki/File:Western_Zhou_Bronze_Mao_(Spear)_(9925396204).jpg

[14] *Mx. Granger, CC0, via Wikimedia Commons:*
https://commons.wikimedia.org/wiki/File:Statue_of_Confucius_at_Beijing_temple.JPG

[15] *Mary Harrsch, CC BY-SA 4.0 <https://creativecommons.org/licenses/by-sa/4.0>, via Wikimedia Commons:*
https://commons.wikimedia.org/wiki/File:Jar_(guan)_ceramic_stoneware_Warring_States_period_(475-221_BCE_Zhou_Dynasty_(1046-256_BCE)_Zhejiang_Province_China.jpg

[16] *Gary Todd, CC0, via Wikimedia Commons:*
https://commons.wikimedia.org/wiki/File:Western_Zhou_Iron_Sword_with_Jade_Handle.jpg

[17] *Thanato, CC BY-SA 3.0 <https://creativecommons.org/licenses/by-sa/3.0>, via Wikimedia Commons: https://commons.wikimedia.org/wiki/File:Laozi_002.jpg*

[18] *Gary Todd, CC0, via Wikimedia Commons:*
https://commons.wikimedia.org/wiki/File:Middle_Western_Zhou_Bronze_%22Li%22_Zun_inscriptions.jpg

[19] *Huangdan2060, CC0, via Wikimedia Commons:*
https://commons.wikimedia.org/wiki/File:Bronze_helmet,_Warring_States_period,_Henan_Museum.jpg

[20] *Gary Lee Todd, Ph.D., CC0, via Wikimedia Commons*
https://commons.wikimedia.org/wiki/File:Western_Zhou_Jade_13.jpg

[21] *Gary Lee Todd, Ph.D., CC0, via Wikimedia Commons:*
https://commons.wikimedia.org/wiki/File:Qin_Terracotta_Warriors_09.jpg

[22] *Photo by CEphoto, Uwe Aranas:*
https://commons.wikimedia.org/wiki/File:Xian_China_Terracotta-Army-Museum-04.jpg

[23] *https://commons.wikimedia.org/wiki/File:Qinshihuang.jpg*

[24] *Jakub Hałun, CC BY-SA 3.0 <https://creativecommons.org/licenses/by-sa/3.0>, via Wikimedia Commons: https://commons.wikimedia.org/wiki/File:20090529_Great_Wall_8185.jpg*

[25] *https://commons.wikimedia.org/wiki/File:Liu-bang.jpg*

[26] *Neil Satyam, CC BY-SA 3.0 <https://creativecommons.org/licenses/by-sa/3.0>, via Wikimedia Commons: https://commons.wikimedia.org/wiki/File:80_feet_Buddha_Statue_-_panoramio_(4).jpg*

[27]
https://commons.wikimedia.org/wiki/File:Fresco_of_a_Horseman_from_a_Han_Dynasty_Tomb_in_Sian,_Shensi.jpg

[28] *User: Captmondo, CC BY-SA 3.0 <http://creativecommons.org/licenses/by-sa/3.0/>, via Wikimedia Commons: https://commons.wikimedia.org/wiki/File:QueenMotherOfTheWest-Earthenware-EasternHanDynasty-ROM-May8-08.png*

[29] *Gary Todd, CC0, via Wikimedia Commons:*
https://commons.wikimedia.org/wiki/File:Eastern_Han_Pottery_Tower_-_2a.jpg

[30] *Gary Todd from Xinzheng, China, CC0, via Wikimedia Commons:*
https://commons.wikimedia.org/wiki/File:Western_Han_Bronze_%26_Gold_Chariot_Ornament_(10129135603).jpg

[31] *Gary Todd, CC0, via Wikimedia Commons:*
https://commons.wikimedia.org/wiki/File:Tang_Dynasty_Amitabha_Buddha.jpg

[32] *https://commons.wikimedia.org/wiki/File:A_Tang_poem_in_praise_of_chrysanthemums.jpg*

[33] *Gary Todd, CC0, via Wikimedia Commons:*
https://commons.wikimedia.org/wiki/File:Tang_White_Porcelain_Lampstand.jpg

[34] *Flickr user Gary Todd, CC BY-SA 4.0 <https://creativecommons.org/licenses/by-sa/4.0>, via Wikimedia Commons: https://commons.wikimedia.org/wiki/File:Tang_Silk_Painting_02.jpg*

[35] *Gary Todd from Xinzheng, China, CC0, via Wikimedia Commons:*
https://commons.wikimedia.org/wiki/File:Tang_Sancai_Glazed_Porcelain_Camel_(10233931985).jpg

[36] *Wmpearl, CC0, via Wikimedia Commons:*
https://commons.wikimedia.org/wiki/File:Military_figures,_Northern_Song_dynasty,_11th_century,_Lowe_Art_Museum.JPG

[37] *https://commons.wikimedia.org/wiki/File:Sitting_Portrait_of_Song_Dynasty_Empress_Xiang.jpg*

[38] *Gary Todd, CC0, via Wikimedia Commons:*
https://commons.wikimedia.org/wiki/File:Grave_Offerings_5_-_Tang_Sancai_Porcelain_Horse_%26_Attendant.jpg

[39] *John E. Sandrock, Public domain, via Wikimedia Commons:*
https://commons.wikimedia.org/wiki/File:Hue-tzu_(Song_Dynasty_government_issue),_1023_-_John_E._Sandrock.jpg

[40] *Gary Lee Todd, CC BY-SA 4.0 <https://creativecommons.org/licenses/by-sa/4.0>, via Wikimedia Commons: https://commons.wikimedia.org/wiki/File:Song_Dynasty_porcelain_pillow2.JPG*

[41] *INTERFOTO/Fine Arts, CC BY-SA 4.0 <https://creativecommons.org/licenses/by-sa/4.0>, via Wikimedia Commons:*
https://commons.wikimedia.org/wiki/File:Yuan_Dynasty_Military_Banners.jpg

[42] *https://commons.wikimedia.org/wiki/File:YuanEmperorAlbumKhubilaiPortrait.jpg*

[43] *https://commons.wikimedia.org/wiki/File:Marco_Polo_Mosaic_from_Palazzo_Tursi.jpg*

[44] *Mary Harrsch, CC BY-SA 4.0 <https://creativecommons.org/licenses/by-sa/4.0>, via Wikimedia Commons:*
https://commons.wikimedia.org/wiki/File:Glazed_porcelain_sculpture_of_seated_bodhisattva_probably_14th_century_CE_Yuan_Dynasty_(1279-1368_CE)_Jiangxi_Province_China.jpg

[45] *Gary Todd, CC0, via Wikimedia Commons:*
https://commons.wikimedia.org/wiki/File:Yuan_Paper_Currency.jpg

[46] *Mary Harrsch, CC BY-SA 4.0 <https://creativecommons.org/licenses/by-sa/4.0>, via Wikimedia Commons: https://commons.wikimedia.org/wiki/File:Guanyin_(Avalokiteshvara)_Yuan-early_Ming_dynasty_late_14th_century_CE.jpg*

[47] *Gary Todd, CC0, via Wikimedia Commons:*
https://commons.wikimedia.org/wiki/File:Yuan_Bronze_Cannon.jpg

[48] *John Hill, CC BY-SA 3.0 <https://creativecommons.org/licenses/by-sa/3.0>, via Wikimedia Commons: https://commons.wikimedia.org/wiki/File:Brown-glazed_Jar_with_Design_of_Three_Fish._Yuan_Dynasty._Excavated_from_Hancheng_City.jpg*

[49] *BossGavinV, CC BY-SA 4.0 <https://creativecommons.org/licenses/by-sa/4.0>, via Wikimedia Commons: https://commons.wikimedia.org/wiki/File:Flag_of_The_Mongol_Empire_3.png*

[50] *Gary Todd, CC0, via Wikimedia Commons: https://commons.wikimedia.org/wiki/File:Yuan_Jade_Belt_Hook.jpg*

[51] *Cattette, CC BY 4.0 <https://creativecommons.org/licenses/by/4.0>, via Wikimedia Commons: https://commons.wikimedia.org/wiki/File:Yuan_Dynasty_revised.png*

[52]

https://commons.wikimedia.org/wiki/File:%E6%98%8E%E5%A4%AA%E7%A5%96%E7%94%BB%E5%83%8F.jpg

[53] *Patrick20242023, CC BY-SA 4.0 <https://creativecommons.org/licenses/by-sa/4.0>, via Wikimedia Commons: https://commons.wikimedia.org/wiki/File:%E8%BE%B9%E9%9D%96%E6%A5%BC%E5%8C%97%E9%9D%A2.jpg*

[54] *J Aaron Farr, CC BY 2.0 <https://creativecommons.org/licenses/by/2.0>, via Wikimedia Commons: https://commons.wikimedia.org/wiki/File:Beijing_Ming_City_Wall_Bastion.jpg*

[55] *Steve46814, CC BY-SA 4.0 <https://creativecommons.org/licenses/by-sa/4.0>, via Wikimedia Commons: https://commons.wikimedia.org/wiki/File:Beijing_Ancient_Observatory_5.jpg*

[56] *Gary Todd from Xinzheng, China, CC0, via Wikimedia Commons: https://commons.wikimedia.org/wiki/File:Zheng_He_Treasure_Ship_(15832736462).jpg*

[57] *User:kallgan, CC BY-SA 3.0 <http://creativecommons.org/licenses/by-sa/3.0/>, via Wikimedia Commons: https://commons.wikimedia.org/wiki/File:Sunset_of_the_Forbidden_City_2006.JPG*

[58] *Stefan Fussan, CC BY-SA 3.0 <https://creativecommons.org/licenses/by-sa/3.0>, via Wikimedia Commons: https://commons.wikimedia.org/wiki/File:Shanghai_-_Yu_Garden_-_0035.jpg*

[59] *Hugh Llewelyn from Keynsham, UK, CC BY-SA 2.0 <https://creativecommons.org/licenses/by-sa/2.0>, via Wikimedia Commons: https://commons.wikimedia.org/wiki/File:The_Thirteen_Tombs_of_the_Ming_Dynasty,_Beijing_(50601402452).jpg*

[60] *danmairen, CC BY-SA 3.0 <https://creativecommons.org/licenses/by-sa/3.0>, via Wikimedia Commons: https://commons.wikimedia.org/wiki/File:Zhihua_Temple_-_panoramio_-_danmairen_(2).jpg*

[61] *钉钉, CC BY-SA 4.0 <https://creativecommons.org/licenses/by-sa/4.0>, via Wikimedia Commons: https://commons.wikimedia.org/wiki/File:Great_Bao%27en_Temple,_Nanjing.jpg*

[62] *Cleveland Museum of Art, CC0, via Wikimedia Commons: https://commons.wikimedia.org/wiki/File:Northern_China,_Liao_dynasty_-_Pair_of_Boots_-_1993.158_-_Cleveland_Museum_of_Art.tif*

[63] *User:PericlesofAthens, CC BY-SA 4.0 <https://creativecommons.org/licenses/by-sa/4.0>, via Wikimedia Commons: https://commons.wikimedia.org/wiki/File:Earthenware_figures_playing_liubo,_Han_Dynasty.JPG*

[64] *Jaki4594, CC BY-SA 3.0 <https://creativecommons.org/licenses/by-sa/3.0>, via Wikimedia Commons: https://commons.wikimedia.org/wiki/File:A_small_house_with_ancient_chinese_architecture.jpg*

---

⁶⁵ Gary Todd, CC0, via Wikimedia Commons:
https://commons.wikimedia.org/wiki/File:Chinese_Wedding_Procession_2.jpg

⁶⁶ Thomas Quine, CC BY 2.0 <https://creativecommons.org/licenses/by/2.0>, via Wikimedia Commons:
https://commons.wikimedia.org/wiki/File:Funeral_litter_found_in_ancient_Chinese_tomb_(46801607464).jpg

⁶⁷ https://commons.wikimedia.org/wiki/File:The_four_classes_of_society_by_Ozawa_Nankoku.jpeg

⁶⁸ mararie from Brookline, United States, CC BY-SA 2.0 <https://creativecommons.org/licenses/by-sa/2.0>, via Wikimedia Commons:
https://commons.wikimedia.org/wiki/File:Ancient_glass_chinese_chess_set_(5051064592).jpg

⁶⁹ en:user: Kowloonese, CC BY-SA 3.0 <http://creativecommons.org/licenses/by-sa/3.0/>, via Wikimedia Commons: https://commons.wikimedia.org/wiki/File:EastHanSeismograph.JPG

⁷⁰ Gary Todd from Xinzheng, China, CC0, via Wikimedia Commons:
https://commons.wikimedia.org/wiki/File:Arrows_with_Gunpowder_(9884447845).jpg

⁷¹ Oto Zapletal, CC BY 4.0 <https://creativecommons.org/licenses/by/4.0>, via Wikimedia Commons: https://commons.wikimedia.org/wiki/File:Two_wheelbarrows.jpg

⁷² DLG Images, CC BY 2.0 <https://creativecommons.org/licenses/by/2.0>, via Wikimedia Commons: https://commons.wikimedia.org/wiki/File:Red_Umbrella_1.jpg

⁷³ Alexandramander, CC BY-SA 4.0 <https://creativecommons.org/licenses/by-sa/4.0>, via Wikimedia Commons:
https://commons.wikimedia.org/wiki/File:Yin_and_yang_with_yin_to_the_left.png

⁷⁴ Thomas Nordwest, CC BY-SA 4.0 <https://creativecommons.org/licenses/by-sa/4.0>, via Wikimedia Commons: https://commons.wikimedia.org/wiki/File:Buddha_in_Meditation_2023-05-11-22.jpg

⁷⁵ Brett Vachon from Montreal, Canada, CC BY 2.0 <https://creativecommons.org/licenses/by/2.0>, via Wikimedia Commons:
https://commons.wikimedia.org/wiki/File:Entrance_to_Temple_of_Confucius,_Qufu,_China_(29859087771).jpg

⁷⁶ Zgpdszz, CC BY-SA 3.0 <https://creativecommons.org/licenses/by-sa/3.0>, via Wikimedia Commons:
https://commons.wikimedia.org/wiki/File:Spring_Temple_Buddha_picturing_Vairocana,_in_Lushan_County,_Henan,_China.png

⁷⁷ AlexHe34, CC BY-SA 3.0 <https://creativecommons.org/licenses/by-sa/3.0>, via Wikimedia Commons:
https://commons.wikimedia.org/wiki/File:Commentaries_of_the_Analects_of_Confucius.jpg

⁷⁸ Omer Farooq, CC BY-SA 3.0 <https://creativecommons.org/licenses/by-sa/3.0>, via Wikimedia Commons: https://commons.wikimedia.org/wiki/File:Silk_Route_by_the_side_of_Indus_River.jpg

⁷⁹ https://commons.wikimedia.org/wiki/File:(Ferdinand_von_Richthofen)_-_Ernst_(...)Milster_Ernst_btv1b84510245_(cropped).jpg

⁸⁰ VK Cheong, CC BY-SA 3.0 <https://creativecommons.org/licenses/by-sa/3.0>, via Wikimedia Commons: https://commons.wikimedia.org/wiki/File:Tang_-_Ferghana_War_Horse.JPG

[81] *Christopher from Shanghai, China, CC BY 2.0 <https://creativecommons.org/licenses/by/2.0>, via Wikimedia Commons: https://commons.wikimedia.org/wiki/File:Colorful_Spices_and_Teas.jpg*

[82] *Kaidor, CC BY-SA 4.0 <https://creativecommons.org/licenses/by-sa/4.0>, via Wikimedia Commons: https://commons.wikimedia.org/wiki/File:Silk_Road_in_the_I_century_AD_-_en.svg*

[83] *lensnmatter, Public domain, via Wikimedia Commons: https://commons.wikimedia.org/wiki/File:Spice!_(45645850944).jpg*

[84] *Party Fabrics, CC BY-SA 2.0 <https://creativecommons.org/licenses/by-sa/2.0>, via Wikimedia Commons: https://commons.wikimedia.org/wiki/File:China_silk-crystalblue.jpg*

[85] *Hiart, CC0, via Wikimedia Commons: https://commons.wikimedia.org/wiki/File:Chinese_wine_ewer,_Ming_dynasty,_early_15th_century,_porcelain_with_glaze,_Honolulu_Academy_of_Arts.JPG*

[86] *Editor at Large, CC BY-SA 2.5 <https://creativecommons.org/licenses/by-sa/2.5>, via Wikimedia Commons: https://commons.wikimedia.org/wiki/File:CMOC_Treasures_of_Ancient_China_exhibit_-_jade_disk.jpg*

[87] *Editor at Large, CC BY-SA 2.5 <https://creativecommons.org/licenses/by-sa/2.5>, via Wikimedia Commons: https://commons.wikimedia.org/wiki/File:Ancient_Chinese_Writing_on_Western_Zhou_Bronze_Lai_Plate.jpg*